EYEWITNESS

CLIMATE CHANGE

Geostationary Operational
Environmental Satellite (GOES-17)

Hurricane
structure

Beef burger

Arctic ivory gull

Mammoth

Bus running
on biofuel

Zero-emission
transportation

Carbon dioxide
(CO_2) molecule

Nitrous oxide
(N_2O) molecule

Water vapor
(H_2O) molecule

Methane (CH_4)
molecule

Ozone (O_3)
molecule

Recycling bins

EYEWITNESS

CLIMATE CHANGE

AUTHOR **JOHN WOODWARD**

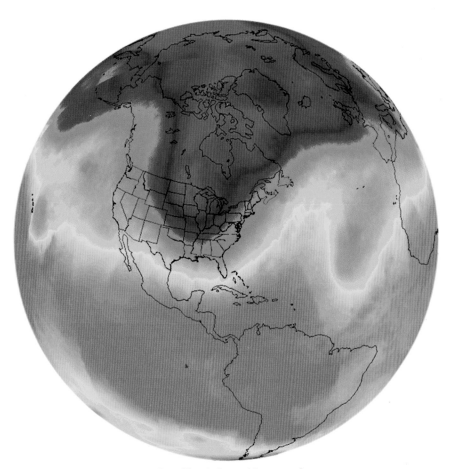

Satellite infrared image of
Earth's temperature

Penguin
Random
House

REVISED EDITION

DK LONDON
Senior Editors Carron Brown, Camilla Hallinan
Senior Art Editor Lynne Moulding
US Editor Heather Wilcox
US Executive Editor Lori Cates Hand
Managing Editor Francesca Baines
Managing Art Editor Philip Letsu
Production Editor George Nimmo
Production Controller Samantha Cross
Jacket Design Development Manager Sophia MTT
Publisher Andrew Macintyre
Associate Publishing Director Liz Wheeler
Art Director Karen Self
Publishing Director Jonathan Metcalf

Consultant Daniel Hooke

DK DELHI
Senior Editor Shatarupa Chaudhuri
Senior Art Editor Vikas Chauhan
Art Editors Baibhav Parida, Sanya Jain
Assistant Editor Sai Prasanna
Project Picture Researcher Deepak Negi
Managing Editor Kingshuk Ghoshal
Managing Art Editor Govind Mittal
Senior DTP Designer Neeraj Bhatia
DTP Designer Pawan Kumar
Jacket Designer Juhi Sheth

FIRST EDITION

DK LONDON
Consultant Dr Piers Forster
Project Editor Margaret Hynes
Managing Editor Camilla Hallinan
Managing Art Editor Owen Peyton Jones
Art Director Martin Wilson
Publishing Manager Sunita Gahir
Category Publisher Andrea Pinnington
Picture Researcher Sarah & Roland Smithies
DK Picture Library Lucy Claxton, Rose Horridge,
Myriam Megharbi, Emma Shepherd, Romaine Werblow
Production Editor Hitesh Patel
Senior Production Controller Man Fai Lau
Jacket Designer Neal Cobourne
Jacket Editor Rob Houston

DK DELHI
Art Director Shefali Upadhyay
Designers Govind Mittal, Tannishtha Chakraborti
DTP Designer Harish Aggarwal

This Eyewitness ® Book has been conceived by
Dorling Kindersley Limited and Editions Gallimard

This American Edition, 2021
First American Edition, 2008
Published in the United States by DK Publishing
1450 Broadway, Suite 801, New York, NY 10018

Copyright © 2008, 2011, 2021
Dorling Kindersley Limited
DK, a Division of Penguin Random House LLC
21 22 23 24 25 10 9 8 7 6 5 4 3 2 1
001–323215–Aug/2021

A catalog record for this book is available from the Library of Congress.
ISBN: 978-0-7440-3906-1 (Paperback)
ISBN: 978-0-7440-3681-7 (ALB)

DK books are available at special discounts when purchased in bulk
for sales promotions, premiums, fund-raising, or educational use.
For details, contact: DK Publishing Special Markets,
1450 Broadway, Suite 801, New York, NY 10018
SpecialSales@dk.com

Printed and bound in UAE

For the curious
www.dk.com

MIX
Paper from
responsible sources
FSC™ C018179

This book was made with Forest Stewardship Council™ certified
paper—one small step in DK's commitment to a sustainable future.
For more information go to www.dk.com/our-green-pledge

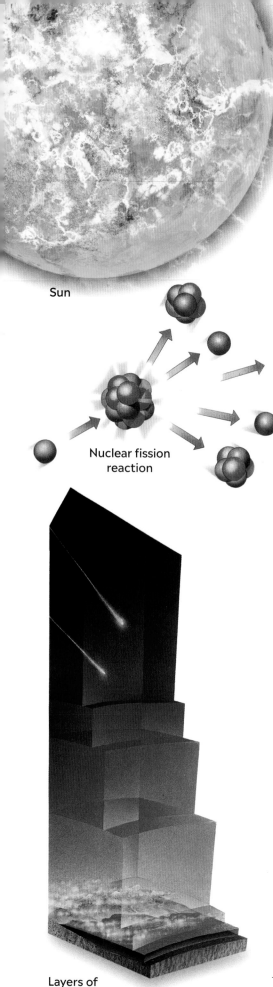

Sun

Nuclear fission
reaction

Layers of
Earth's atmosphere

Fungi

Gas pump

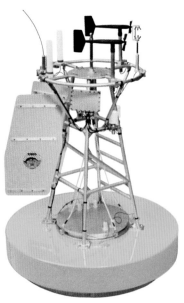

Research buoy

Contents

Planting trees

Earth's climate

Currents in Earth's atmosphere and oceans carry heat and moisture around the globe, sustaining life. These currents also create the weather. The long-term pattern of weather in a particular place is its climate. Climates vary slowly over time, forcing life to adapt to new conditions, but recently the rate of climate change has speeded up.

Living planet
Earth's atmosphere acts like an insulating blanket, keeping temperatures within the limits that allow life to survive.

Barren desert
Liquid water is vital to living things, so regions where any water is either permanently frozen or dried up by the sun are lifeless deserts. In a hot desert like this one in Israel, a slight rise in average temperature could wipe out all traces of life.

Teeming with life
Where the climate is warm and wet, rich ecosystems such as this rain forest provide food for a huge variety of animals. They have all evolved to flourish in the conditions created by a particular type of climate, and many may not be able to survive rapid climate change.

Warming world
Global average temperatures started rising around 1900. They have risen and fallen many times since then, but the trend has crept upward. This matches the rise of modern industry, cities, and increasing consumption of fuel such as coal and oil to provide energy for heating, electrical power, and transportation.

High-altitude jet streams blow east

Earth spins toward the east

Moving weather systems transfer water from the oceans to the continents

Changing climate

Scientists are studying Earth's climate across the world, including Antarctica, as seen here. They have shown that for most of human history, the climate has been stable, enabling civilizations to rise and prosper. But since 1900, the climate has been changing.

TILTED EARTH

The sun shines directly on the tropics around the equator, with a concentrated energy that creates tropical climates. Sunlight strikes the poles at an angle, dispersing its energy and allowing ice sheets to form. The spinning Earth is tilted on its axis, so as Earth orbits the sun each year, the sun's rays heat the north more intensely during the northern summer and the south during the northern winter, creating annual seasons.

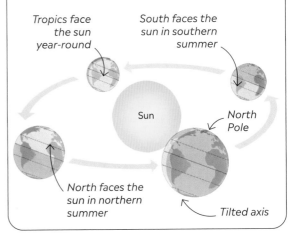

Tropics face the sun year-round

South faces the sun in southern summer

Sun

North Pole

North faces the sun in northern summer

Tilted axis

Atmospheric cell

Earth's rotation makes temperate winds swerve east

Sinking dry air creates deserts

Swirling currents

Intense sunlight in the tropics generates warm air currents that flow towards the poles in a series of rising and sinking "cells." This cools the tropics and warms the temperate and polar regions, giving the planet a more even climate. Winds and weather systems driven by high-altitude air currents also carry moisture from the oceans over the continents, where it falls as rain or snow. This provides the vital water that allows life to flourish on land. Variations in temperature and rainfall create a variety of climate zones, such as deserts and rain forests.

Rising warm, moist air near the equator causes rain over the tropics

👁 EYEWITNESS

Svante Arrhenius
In the 1890s, this Swedish chemist decided that past ice ages might have been caused by fewer volcanic eruptions pumping gases such as carbon dioxide into the atmosphere. He thought that producing more of these gases— by burning fuels, such as coal—would make the world warm up.

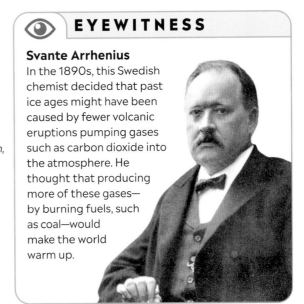

Earth's rotation makes tropical winds swerve west

The greenhouse **effect**

The atmosphere that surrounds our planet acts as both sunscreen and insulation, shielding life from the fiercest of the sun's rays while retaining heat that would otherwise escape back into space at night. This feature of the atmosphere is known as the greenhouse effect. Life on Earth would be impossible without it, but its increasing power is also causing global warming.

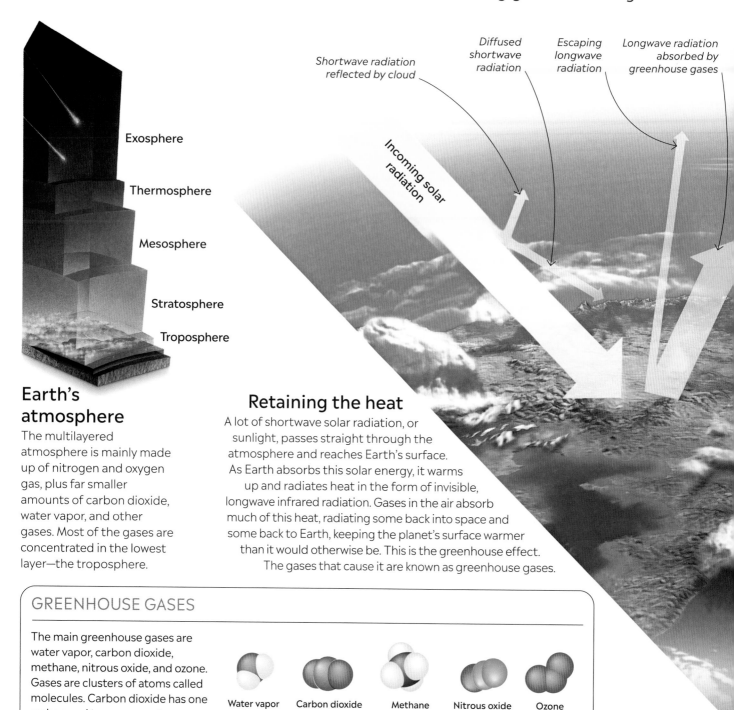

Exosphere

Thermosphere

Mesosphere

Stratosphere

Troposphere

Shortwave radiation reflected by cloud

Diffused shortwave radiation

Escaping longwave radiation

Longwave radiation absorbed by greenhouse gases

Incoming solar radiation

Earth's atmosphere

The multilayered atmosphere is mainly made up of nitrogen and oxygen gas, plus far smaller amounts of carbon dioxide, water vapor, and other gases. Most of the gases are concentrated in the lowest layer—the troposphere.

Retaining the heat

A lot of shortwave solar radiation, or sunlight, passes straight through the atmosphere and reaches Earth's surface. As Earth absorbs this solar energy, it warms up and radiates heat in the form of invisible, longwave infrared radiation. Gases in the air absorb much of this heat, radiating some back into space and some back to Earth, keeping the planet's surface warmer than it would otherwise be. This is the greenhouse effect. The gases that cause it are known as greenhouse gases.

GREENHOUSE GASES

The main greenhouse gases are water vapor, carbon dioxide, methane, nitrous oxide, and ozone. Gases are clusters of atoms called molecules. Carbon dioxide has one carbon and two oxygen atoms.

Water vapor (H_2O)

Carbon dioxide (CO_2)

Methane (CH_4)

Nitrous oxide (N_2O)

Ozone (O_3)

Life support

Without Earth's atmosphere, temperatures would be scorching by day and plunge to far below freezing at night. The average global temperature would sink from 57°F (14°C) to about 0°F (–18°C). Without the greenhouse effect, life on Earth could not have evolved.

Like any living being, the rose plant will die if temperatures remain freezing.

Cold neighbor

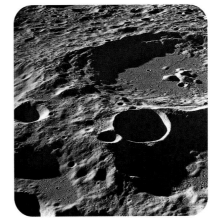

The moon is a lot smaller than Earth and has lower gravity, so any gas seeping from its interior drifts into space instead of forming an atmosphere. With no greenhouse effect, the surface temperature is far lower—one reason why there is no life there.

Heat escapes into space

Warm gases heat Earth's surface

Greenhouse gases in the atmosphere

Charles Keeling

Measurements of carbon dioxide (CO_2) in the air by American scientist Charles Keeling show that its concentration has been increasing every year since 1958. CO_2 absorbs a lot less energy per molecule than the other greenhouse gases, but there is much more of it.

Greenhouse planet

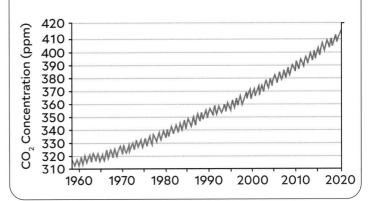

Venus is the same size as Earth and has an atmosphere, but it is too close to the sun for oceans to form. On Earth, oceans absorb carbon dioxide from the air, reducing the greenhouse effect. But on Venus, with no oceans, a hugely powerful greenhouse effect raises the average surface temperature to above 930°F (500°C)—hot enough to melt lead.

KEELING'S CURVE

Keeling's atmospheric carbon-dioxide measurements create a rising zigzag line on a graph. The zigzag effect indicates the seasonal rise and fall due to the absorption of CO_2 by plants growing on the vast northern continents in summer. But the trend of the graph keeps rising, from 315 parts of CO_2 per million parts of air in 1958 to 411 in 2019.

CO$_2$ Concentration (ppm) — 420, 410, 400, 390, 380, 370, 360, 350, 340, 330, 320, 310 — 1960, 1970, 1980, 1990, 2000, 2010, 2020

The carbon cycle

When carbon combines with oxygen, it forms carbon dioxide (CO_2). Green plants absorb CO_2 from the air during photosynthesis, fueling life processes. During respiration, plants release CO_2 back into the air. CO_2 is also released through burning and decay, absorbed and released by the oceans, and erupted from volcanoes. So carbon is continually passing between living things, the atmosphere, oceans, and rocks—an exchange called the carbon cycle.

CO_2 and methane return to atmosphere

Water evaporates, drawing more water up the stem

Sunlight gathered by green leaves

CO_2 absorbed from air

Photosynthesis

Green plants and marine plankton use solar energy to turn CO_2 and water into sugar. This process, called photosynthesis, also releases oxygen. Sugar stores the energy of the sun in chemical form, and nearly all living things on Earth rely on this energy to build their tissues and fuel their activities. Life is built on carbon.

Oxygen is released into the air

Respiration

Plants and animals use oxygen to release the energy stored in sugar and other carbohydrates. Known as respiration, this turns the sugar back into CO_2 and water. Animals breathe in the oxygen and breathe out to lose CO_2 and water vapor.

Water flows up stem to leaves

Water drawn up from soil by roots

Breath seen as a misty cloud on a cold day

Worms feed on dead plants and animals and release CO_2

The carbon cycle

Carbon is constantly being absorbed and released by living things. Plants and other photosynthesizers absorb CO_2 and use some of the carbon to build their tissues. The carbon is released as CO_2 or methane when plants die and decay. If animals eat the plants, they use some of the carbon to build their own tissues but eventually die too. Meanwhile, both plants and animals release CO_2 when they turn sugar into energy by respiration.

Growing plants absorb CO_2 for photosynthesis

Plants release some CO_2 by respiration, but less than they absorb

Animals produce CO_2 and methane

Animals eat plants

Decaying plants, animal remains, and animal waste produce carbon

Organic decay

When living things die, other organisms such as bacteria and these fungi start recycling their basic ingredients. This process of decay often combines the carbon in the dead tissues with oxygen, so it returns to the atmosphere as CO_2. Another type of decay combines the carbon with hydrogen to form methane.

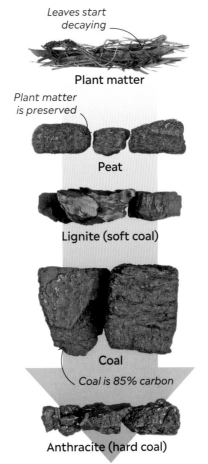

CARBON STORAGE

When a plant or animal dies, it usually starts decaying right away, and its carbon content soon returns to the air. But sometimes it is buried in such a way that it does not decay properly. Dead plants that sink into a waterlogged bog often do not rot away but turn into deep layers of peat. Eventually, the peat may be compressed into coal, a process that stores the carbon for millions of years.

Leaves start decaying

Plant matter

Plant matter is preserved

Peat

Lignite (soft coal)

Coal

Coal is 85% carbon

Anthracite (hard coal)

Volcanic carbon

Carbon stored in the rocks of Earth's crust is returned to the atmosphere by volcanoes. They erupt both molten rock and gases, which include CO_2 released by carbonate rocks, such as limestones, as they melt. Small amounts of CO_2 erupt from volcanoes every year and are gradually absorbed by the formation of more carbonate rocks.

Temperature control

During Earth's early history, 3.5 billion years ago, CO_2 erupting from volcanoes created an intense greenhouse effect that prevented Earth from freezing. Over time, the sun grew hotter, but most of the erupted CO_2 was soaked up by the oceans (below), reducing the greenhouse effect at roughly the same rate— evidence that Earth may be a self-regulating system.

Checks and balances

The energy that Earth soaks up from the sun is more or less balanced by the energy that it radiates out into space. However, imbalances caused by greenhouse gases can make the planet colder or warmer, leading to other changes in the climate system known as feedbacks. Scientists are concerned that a large rise in global temperature may trigger powerful feedbacks that will continue to make Earth warmer.

Carbon uptake

One of the main checks on the greenhouse effect involves plants and marine plankton, as the more CO_2 there is, the faster they grow and the more CO_2 they absorb. Here, plants are being grown in a sealed enclosure containing extra CO_2 to see how they respond.

Earth's energy balance

When sunlight strikes Earth's atmosphere, about a third of its energy—shown here in watts per square meter—is returned to space by reflection from clouds, tiny airborne particles called aerosols, and Earth's surface. More energy is absorbed by the atmosphere, leaving less than half to be absorbed by the sea and land. These warm up and radiate heat energy back into the atmosphere, where some is trapped by greenhouse gases.

Shortwave and longwave radiation

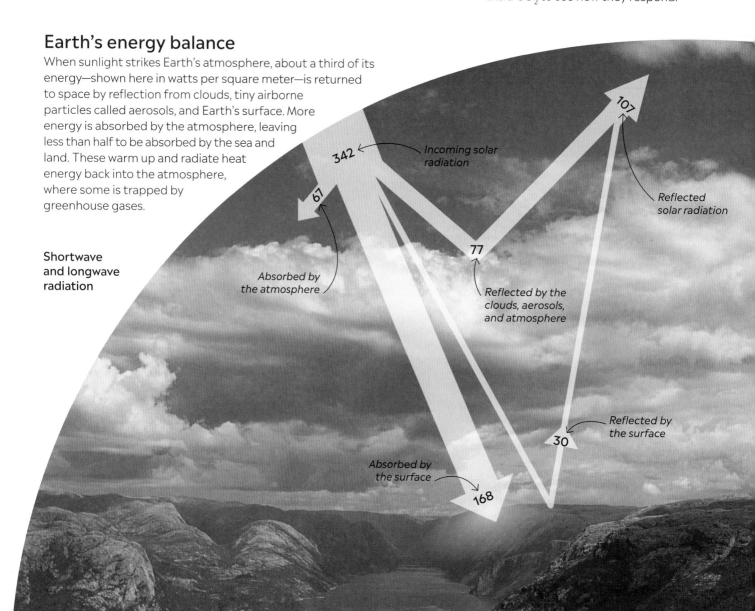

342 — Incoming solar radiation

107 — Reflected solar radiation

67 — Absorbed by the atmosphere

77 — Reflected by the clouds, aerosols, and atmosphere

30 — Reflected by the surface

168 — Absorbed by the surface

Positive feedbacks

When ice forms or snow falls, the dazzling white surface acts like a mirror. It reflects solar energy, so less heat is absorbed by the ground and more ice forms. This is called the albedo effect. It is an example of positive feedback, which magnifies the initial imbalance, leading to greater temperature change.

Negative feedbacks

Some natural processes resist change. When intense sunlight warms the ocean surface, water evaporates and rises into the air as water vapor. As it rises, it cools and forms clouds, which shade the ocean so it cools down. Eventually, evaporation and cloud formation stop, so sunlight can warm the ocean again.

Tipping points

If a jug full of ice cubes is warmed up from 14°F (–10°C) at the rate of a degree or two an hour, nothing happens until just above 32°F (0°C). Then, all the ice cubes start melting. Rising global temperatures may pass similar tipping points, causing sudden changes and triggering positive feedbacks that will accelerate the process.

| 14°F (–10°C) | 23°F (–5°C) | 30°F (–1°C) | 32°F (0°C) | 34°F (1°C) |

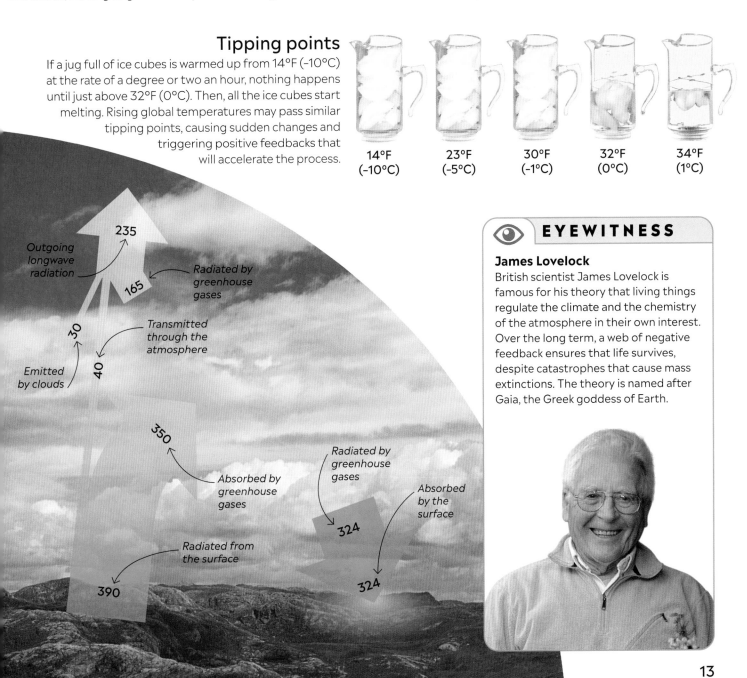

235
Outgoing longwave radiation

Radiated by greenhouse gases
165

30

Transmitted through the atmosphere
40

Emitted by clouds

350
Absorbed by greenhouse gases

Radiated by greenhouse gases

Absorbed by the surface

324

Radiated from the surface

390

324

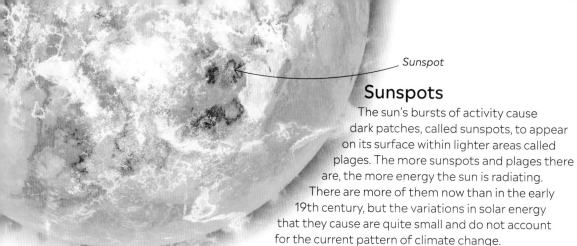

Sunspot

Sunspots

The sun's bursts of activity cause dark patches, called sunspots, to appear on its surface within lighter areas called plages. The more sunspots and plages there are, the more energy the sun is radiating. There are more of them now than in the early 19th century, but the variations in solar energy that they cause are quite small and do not account for the current pattern of climate change.

Natural climate change

The current rise in average global temperature is being caused by human activities. But climate change has also occurred in the past, even before people existed and started to change the world. These shifts were caused by natural cycles that affect Earth's orbit around the sun, by changes in solar radiation levels, and by catastrophic natural events, such as massive volcanic eruptions.

Geological evidence

Clues to changing climate can be found in rocks. Thick layers of red sandstone in northern Europe were once sand dunes that built up in hot deserts. The thick white chalk rock at the top of this English cliff was formed in a shallow tropical sea at the time of the dinosaurs.

Continental drift

Over millions of years, the shifting plates of Earth's crust move the continents into new arrangements, changing their climates. Around 250 million years ago, this process created the single, vast "supercontinent" of Pangaea, which had a very dry desert climate because most of the land was so far from the ocean.

Chalk formed millions of years ago

Volcanic eruptions

Some volcanic eruptions propel dust and gases high into the stratosphere. There, sulfuric acid can drift for years, obscuring the sun and causing global cooling of 1.8°F (1°C) or more. But carbon dioxide stays in the atmosphere for more than a century, causing global warming. Eruptions may have dramatically changed past climates, but recent eruptions have not been big enough.

In June 1991, the huge eruption of Mount Pinatubo in the Philippines spewed sulfur dioxide into the atmosphere, which had a cooling effect on Earth's climate

Maureen Raymo

The American climate scientist Maureen Raymo studies ice ages and why they happen. Her work is important to understanding the difference between climate change that occurs naturally and human-made climate change.

Ice ages

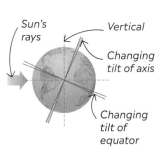

Earth's ice ages are caused by orbital cycles. Today, Earth is in a warm phase, but 20,000 years ago, an ice age was at full strength. Ice sheets covered vast areas of the north, fringed by snowy tundra that was home to cold-adapted animals like this woolly mammoth.

EARTH'S CYCLES

Orbital cycles

Earth's climate changes in cycles caused by variations in its orbit around the sun. One 100,000-year cycle changes the orbit from almost circular to elliptical, affecting our annual temperature range.

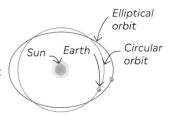

Elliptical orbit

Sun Earth

Circular orbit

Tilted Earth

Every 24 hours, Earth spins around an axis tilted at 23.5° from the vertical. The spin gives us night and day, the tilt our winters and summers. Over a 42,000-year cycle, the tilt varies from 21.6° to 24.5°, changing the areas of the tropical and polar regions and affecting global air circulation.

Sun's rays

Vertical

Changing tilt of axis

Changing tilt of equator

Axis drift

A 25,800-year cycle alters the orientation of Earth's axis, and the poles align with different points in space. Halfway through the cycle, the dates of winter and summer are reversed.

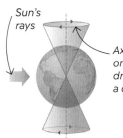

Sun's rays

Axis orientation drifts in a circle

Human impact

The world has warmed by only 7°F (4°C) in the 20,000 years since the peak of the last ice age, but by 2.1°F (1.2°C) since 1900. In that short time, we have enjoyed a technological revolution made possible by a massive consumption of energy. Most of the energy has been generated using fuel that, when burned, releases carbon dioxide (CO_2). The increase in CO_2 matches the rise in global air temperature, so accelerated global warming is being caused by our modern, energy-hungry way of life.

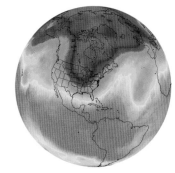
Clues from the past

Scientists drill into the ice of Greenland and Antarctica, extracting samples of ice called ice cores. Bubbles trapped in the ice contain records of previous changes in greenhouse gases. The deepest ice in Antarctica has information about the climate 800,000 years ago.

Ice core is carefully slid out of a hollow drill

Climate scientists at an Antarctic research station

Trapped bubbles

Air gets trapped by snowfall. As more snowfall accumulates, the buildup of pressure gradually turns the snow into ice, with air bubbles caught inside. Scientists measure the CO_2 in these bubbles, which has revealed how much the concentration of this greenhouse gas has changed in the past (shown in the graph at the bottom of the page).

The prime suspect

Air bubbles trapped in ice cores show that the level of CO_2 in the atmosphere in 1700 was roughly 280 ppm, or 280 parts of CO_2 per million of air. Today, air samples taken by devices attached to the top of towers like this one reveal that the level in 2019 was 411 ppm CO_2. The 131-ppm increase has added significantly to the greenhouse effect, and this is why global temperatures have risen and are continuing to rise.

Scientist collecting air samples

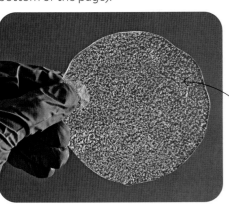

Tiny bubbles trapped in the ice

Arctic ivory gull is threatened by loss of sea ice

Averages and extremes

The 2.1°F (1.2°C) temperature rise over the last 120 years does not sound very serious, but some animals are in decline because of it. The figure is an average of all the local temperature changes all over the world. In some places, the temperature may not have risen at all. But in parts of the Arctic where this gull lives, local winter temperatures have risen by up to 7°F (4°C) since the 1950s, and the ice on which this bird depends for feeding, breeding, and wintering has melted away.

GRAPHIC PROOF

Evidence from ice cores shows that across the ice ages and warm periods of the last 800,000 years, CO_2 has remained between 180 and 300 ppm. The human impact is an increase in CO_2 that is unmatched in natural climate change, causing the planet to warm.

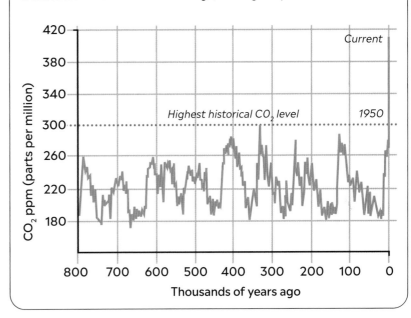

Current

Highest historical CO_2 level   1950

CO₂ ppm (parts per million)

Thousands of years ago

Carbon stores

A growing tree absorbs CO_2 and converts it into sugar, plant fiber, and wood. The wood stores carbon, but when the tree dies and decays, the carbon is released. If a burned forest regrows, the new trees absorb the CO_2 released by the fire. But this may take a century or more, because young trees do not absorb as much CO_2 as mature trees do.

Every year an area of the Amazon rain forest equivalent to one million soccer fields gets cleared.

Slash and burn

Wildfires are part of the natural carbon cycle, and the CO_2 they release is soon absorbed by young trees. But if a forest is felled, burned, and not allowed to regrow, all its carbon is turned into CO_2 that increases the greenhouse effect.

Burning the forests

Most of the extra carbon dioxide (CO_2) that accelerates climate change is being released by burning carbon-rich fuels, including wood, which people have been burning for thousands of years for heat and cooking. As early human civilizations grew larger, the demand for burning wood greatly increased. But vast forests are also being felled and burned to clear land for farming, ranching, and road building, especially in the tropics. This is also contributing to climate change by releasing all the carbon that the forest trees have absorbed over their lifetimes.

Tropical destruction

Tropical rain forests are being cleared by farmers or by large companies to make way for fields for planting, cattle pastures, or new roads and housing. By 2020, 17 percent of the Amazon had been deforested over the past 50 years alone. This aerial view reveals deforestation in Brazil to make space for planting a food crop, cassava.

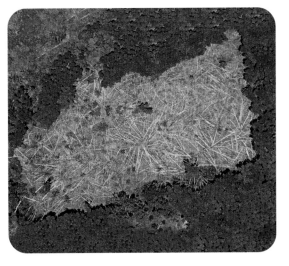

Stripped soil

When a forest is cut down, the bare soil also starts releasing greenhouse gases, such as CO_2 and methane. In Indonesia, the soils of swampy lowland forests contain a lot of waterlogged peat. If the forest is felled, the peat can dry out, decay, and even catch fire, releasing more CO_2.

Aftermath of deforestation by slash and burn in Indonesian rain forest

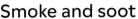

Smoke and soot

Wildfires (seen as red dots in this NASA satellite image) created a smoke screen over Australia in 2019–2020. The smoke is made up of gases and soot that combine with water vapor to form clouds of airborne particles called aerosols. These can absorb and reflect sunlight, causing cooling. But the CO_2 released persists for much longer, adding to the greenhouse effect.

Sustainable fuel

Wood can be used as a "carbon-neutral" fuel if more is grown to replace it. A technique called coppicing involves cutting wood from a living tree and allowing new shoots to sprout from the trunk. When the wood is burned, it releases its carbon as CO_2, but this is absorbed by the regrowing timber.

Fossil fuels

Timber was the world's main fuel for thousands of years, but in the 18th century, people began mining coal, a more concentrated, abundant source of energy. Coal fueled the rise of modern industry and of railways and steamships. Later, oil and natural gas were developed into fuels for road vehicles and aircraft, and both coal and gas are used to generate electricity that powers our modern lives. But burning these carbon-rich "fossil fuels" produces greenhouse gases.

Coal mining

Coal found close to the surface is extracted by open-cast mining, which gouges huge holes in the landscape, such as this one in Wyoming. For underground coal seams, deep shafts lead to tunnels, where miners use special machinery to extract coal.

Fossil fern in coal

Stored sunlight

Fossil fuels are the remains of organisms buried underground before they had time to decay. Coal is made of plants, so it contains the remains of the carbohydrates they created by using the energy of sunlight. So, coal is stored solar energy, compacted over millions of years.

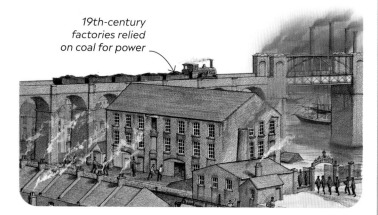

19th-century factories relied on coal for power

Industrial Revolution

Coal transformed industry by providing an abundant, portable source of energy. Manufacturing industries flourished, leading to the growth of towns and cities and liberating people from relying on the land to supply their needs. Coal created modern society but also caused smoke and soot pollution.

 EYEWITNESS

Great Smog of 1952
As it burns, coal produces smoke and pollutants that mix with water vapor to form a smoky fog, called smog. In 1952, a thick smog hung over London for five days, killing up to 12,000 people. As a result, the UK government passed the Clean Air Act in 1956, to restrict the use of coal in industry and the home.

Drilling for oil

The world's first oil well was sunk at Baku on the shores of the Caspian Sea in 1847. But the oil industry did not take off until the early 20th century, when a refined form of oil (petrol) began to be used as a fuel for cars. Today, oil and gas are tapped from reserves all over the world, on land and beneath shallow seas, where it is pumped up from below the sea bed by oil platforms such as this one off the coast of Norway.

Johan Sverdrup
oil field, Norway

Oil and gas

Oil is a hydrocarbon, an organic compound containing only the elements hydrogen and carbon. It is found in rocks that were formed on shallow sea floors and is made up of the remains of marine plankton, such as these microscopic diatoms, which were buried and compressed in the same way as coal-forming plants. The same process that produces oil also creates natural gas, a gas made up of hydrocarbons.

Releasing the energy

Burning coal, or any fossil fuel, releases its energy as heat. But it also combines its carbon with oxygen to form carbon dioxide (CO_2). This accelerates part of the carbon cycle by oxidizing masses of ancient carbon that would naturally be recycled over millions of years. The CO_2 pours into the atmosphere much faster than it can be soaked up by the processes that formed the fuel in the first place, so the concentration of CO_2 in the air increases, adding to the greenhouse effect.

Air travel
Jet aircraft are major producers of carbon dioxide and other greenhouse gases, such as nitrous oxides. Short-haul flights are particularly inefficient because more of the journey is spent gaining height with the engines at full power.

Our carbon culture

Modern society runs on fossil fuels. They power our transportation; run our industries; heat our houses, hospitals, and schools; and generate most of our electricity. Oil is also turned into plastics that are used for everything from food packaging to computers. But our dependence on fossil fuels is the main reason why so much carbon dioxide (CO_2) is being pumped into the atmosphere, increasing the greenhouse effect and causing global warming.

On the road
Nearly all cars run on hydrocarbon fuels—such as gas and diesel—made from oil. Heavy and powerful cars, in particular, use a large amount of fuel. The number of cars is growing worldwide, as they continue to be a popular form of transportation.

Computer age
Computers are powered by electricity, and virtually everything we now do or buy involves computers of some kind. Banks, businesses, and governments rely on electronic communications, as do transportation control rooms like this one.

Power hungry
Coal-fired power plants burn huge amounts of fuel to produce electricity. This plant in Tennessee burns more than 13,800 tons (14,000 metric tons) of coal every day—enough to fill 140 of these big rail trucks—to generate electricity for 700,000 homes.

A flight of 186 miles (300 km) emits up to
12 times as much carbon dioxide, per passenger,
as traveling the same distance by train.

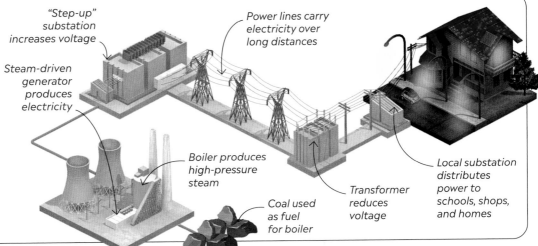

POWER PLANT

A huge proportion of electricity generated in industrialized countries is produced using fossil fuels—64% in the US, for example. In a power plant, the fuel is used to heat a boiler that turns water to steam. The steam is fed to a turbine at high pressure, the spinning turbine turns the electricity generator, and the steam is cooled to turn it back into water for the boiler.

"Step-up" substation increases voltage

Steam-driven generator produces electricity

Power lines carry electricity over long distances

Boiler produces high-pressure steam

Coal used as fuel for boiler

Transformer reduces voltage

Local substation distributes power to schools, shops, and homes

Food miles

A lot of our food comes from abroad. Bananas, for example, grow only in tropical climates, so they have to be imported by cooler countries. Transporting all this food can use a lot of fuel, especially if it arrives by air.

Rail transport

Diesel or diesel-electric trains like this one run on fossil fuel, as do electrified lines that use power generated by burning fossil fuels, including coal. However, railroads use fuel more efficiently than road transportation does, especially when carrying heavy goods, and produce far fewer emissions.

Heat

In cooler climates, many houses have central heating fueled by coal, oil, gas, or electricity. Gas is also widely used for cooking. Some electricity is generated without using fossil fuels, but all the other systems use them and release CO_2, contributing to climate change.

Adding to **the problem**

Deforestation and the use of fossil fuels are not the only human activities causing climate change. Other aspects of modern life are adding to the problem by producing more carbon dioxide (CO_2) as well as other greenhouse gases, such as methane, nitrous oxide, and chlorofluorocarbons (CFCs). These other greenhouse gases are released in much smaller quantities than CO_2, but they have a serious impact because they are much more powerful.

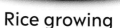

Cement and carbon

Cement is made from limestone that is ground into a powder, releasing CO_2, and then heated to about 2,640°F (1,450°C), which produces emissions. Cement is very heavy, so transporting it also uses a lot of fuel. Altogether, producing and shipping each bag of cement releases roughly the same weight of CO_2 into the atmosphere.

Rice growing

About 10–15 percent of total global methane emissions come from rice fields. Microbes in the wet soil of flooded paddy fields absorb carbon released by rice plants and turn it into methane, which then seeps into the atmosphere.

Nitrous oxide

Although it's a relatively scarce gas, nitrous oxide is about 300 times as powerful as CO_2. While it is produced naturally by bacteria in the soil, exposed soil may release twice the usual amount. It is also released from the artificial fertilizer that farmers spread on their fields.

WARMING FACTORS

This chart shows how much each human-caused greenhouse gas contributes to total emissions around the globe. Warming gases include carbon dioxide (CO_2), methane (CH_4), nitrous oxide (N_2O), artificial gases such as CFCs, and the ground-level ozone that pollution produces (not shown here).

Cattle ranching

Our appetite for beef has caused a big increase in cattle ranching, especially in the tropics. Globally, cattle farming makes up 9 percent of total emissions from human activity. The largest source is methane burped out by cows digesting their food.

Beef burger

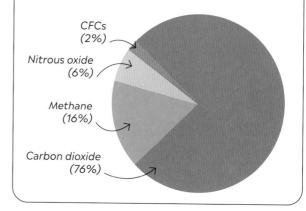

CFCs (2%)

Nitrous oxide (6%)

Methane (16%)

Carbon dioxide (76%)

Surface reflectance

Airborne soot has been carried to the Arctic, where it settles on snow and ice, making it darker so it does not reflect as much sunlight. Instead, it absorbs the energy and warms up. This is helping raise temperatures in the Arctic, melting snow and floating sea ice.

Aerosols

Some forms of air pollution create clouds of small particles known as aerosols. These can reflect or absorb sunlight and reduce its power. This has reduced the impact of the human-enhanced greenhouse effect over recent decades. Ironically, reducing air pollution could accelerate warming.

Chlorofluorocarbons (CFCs)

A variety of artificial gases are now known to be potent greenhouse gases. They include the CFCs that were once used as coolants in refrigerators. When old fridges are discarded, they must have the gas carefully removed to prevent it from escaping into the atmosphere.

Landfill

Developed countries generate immense quantities of trash. A lot of it gets burned, releasing CO_2 and other, more noxious gases. But a lot more is buried in "landfill sites," where food waste and other organic remains are broken down by bacteria. These return carbon to the air in the form of methane, which is an extremely potent greenhouse gas—so even burying trash is helping cause global warming.

Heatwaves
and droughts

By comparing weather and climate data past and present, scientists can calculate how much the world has warmed up. But in many parts of the world, the evidence of climate change is obvious. They are experiencing heatwaves that can raise temperatures to lethal levels and droughts that make drinking water scarce, kill crops and farm animals, and turn fertile land to desert. And these periods of extreme hot or dry weather are getting more frequent.

Drought and famine
Many people living on the fringes of deserts rely on seasonal rains to make their crops grow and provide water for their farm animals. Without enough rain because of changed weather patterns, crops and animals may die, as seen here in southern Ethiopia in 2000. With nothing to eat, people face famine.

Wildfires
Forest fires erupt during very hot, dry weather. In dry regions, many plants can cope with regular fires, but in parts of the Amazon, drought and deforestation are making the ground so dry that wildfires are raging through forests that have never suffered them before.

Heatwaves
Periods of sustained high temperatures can lead to heatwaves, which are becoming more common. During the European heatwave of 2019, Paris suffered from an all-time record temperature of 108.7°F (42.6°C). The UK recorded an all-time high temperature of 101.7°F (38.7°C).

Dried-up rivers

Reduced rainfall is making some rivers dry up. In 2005, the Amazon River suffered its worst drought in 40 years. Many of its tributaries shrank—even the Rio Negro, the main northern tributary, was reduced to its lowest level since records began in 1902.

Desertification

Without enough rain, soil gradually turns to dust. This can be accelerated by poor farming methods. Deforestation, overgrazing, and high winds are causing the rapid expansion of the central Asian Gobi Desert, driving dust storms across huge areas of China and Mongolia.

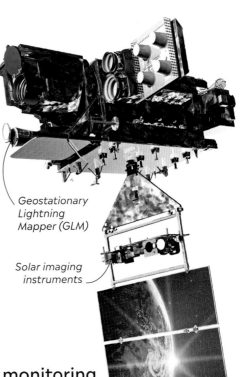

Geostationary Lightning Mapper (GLM)

Solar imaging instruments

Satellite monitoring

Launched in March 2018, the GOES-17 environmental satellite is one of many orbiting spacecraft equipped with remote sensors for monitoring weather in the lower atmosphere, almost 22,370 miles (36,000 km) below the satellite. Scientists compare the satellites' data with past records to determine how much the world has warmed up.

Solar panels provide satellite with electricity

People cooling off at the Trocadéro Garden in Paris, France, during the 2019 heatwave

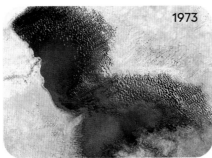

1973

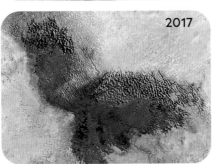

2017

Shrinking lakes

Heat evaporates water from the ground, drying the soil. Without rainfall, the level of groundwater sinks, draining the water from lakes. This becomes worse when people divert water for irrigation. Climate change and irrigation have caused Africa's Lake Chad, once an oasis in the desert, to shrink by 90 percent since the 1960s.

 EYEWITNESS

The human toll

In 2010, Russia experienced its worst heatwave in 130 years. As temperatures soared up to 111.2°F (44°C), wildfires broke out. A thick smog blanketed the city of Moscow (pictured), and people wore face masks for protection. In total, 56,000 people died from both the effects of the smoke and the heatwave.

Melting ice

In cold climates, snow builds up and gradually becomes compacted into ice, forming mountain glaciers and polar ice sheets. Polar oceans also freeze at the surface in winter, creating floating sea ice. However, Arctic sea ice is shrinking, vast Antarctic ice shelves are collapsing, and mountain glaciers are retreating.

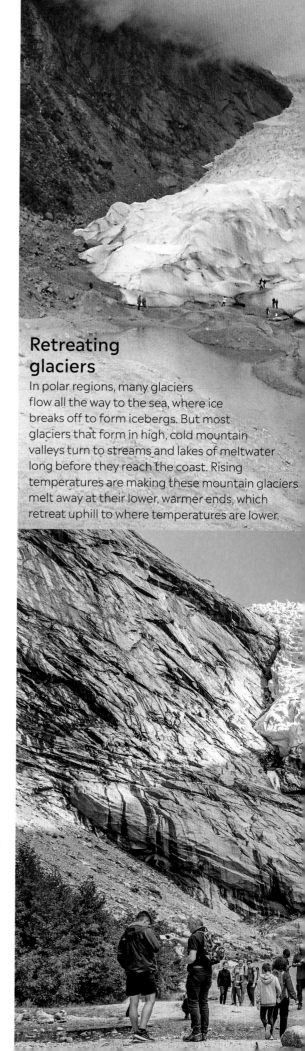

Retreating glaciers

In polar regions, many glaciers flow all the way to the sea, where ice breaks off to form icebergs. But most glaciers that form in high, cold mountain valleys turn to streams and lakes of meltwater long before they reach the coast. Rising temperatures are making these mountain glaciers melt away at their lower, warmer ends, which retreat uphill to where temperatures are lower.

Greenland

Most of Greenland is covered by a huge ice sheet, more than 1.9 miles (3 km) thick at its center. Every summer, the edges of the ice get thinner. The glaciers that flow from the ice sheet to the sea are also moving faster, increasing the rate at which icebergs break away and melt. Both of these processes are causing the sea level to rise.

Accelerating the melt

Glittering white sea ice reflects most of the sun's energy. But if it melts, it gives way to dark patches of ocean water, which absorbs most of the energy and warms up, melting more ice. This positive feedback effect is increasing the rate of Arctic sea ice melting.

Melting permafrost

In the Northern Hemisphere, a quarter of the land is permanently frozen beneath the surface. Above this permafrost is a surface layer that is frozen in winter but thaws in summer, creating vast areas of swampland. In many parts of the lower Arctic, the surface layer is getting deeper each year, melting ancient ice and transforming the tundra landscape.

2002
Briksdal glacier,
Norway

2018
Briksdal glacier,
Norway

Shrinking sea ice

In winter, most of the Arctic Ocean is covered with a sheet of floating ice up to 10 ft (3 m) thick and roughly the size of the United States. Half of this area melts in summer, leaving only the central Arctic Ocean frozen. Since 1979, the size of this summer ice sheet has dwindled by about 1 million sq miles (2.7 million sq km)—an area about four times the size of Texas.

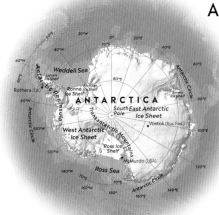

Antarctica

Antarctica is covered by a vast ice sheet up to 2.8 miles (4.5 km) thick, over an area of 5.4 million sq miles (14 million sq km). The huge east Antarctic ice sheet seems to be gaining ice, and the smaller west Antarctic ice sheet is losing ice. The ice is melting fastest on the Antarctic Peninsula, where temperatures are rising more rapidly than elsewhere on Earth, by up to 5.4°F (3°C) since 1951.

👁 EYEWITNESS

Frozen ancestor
In 1991, two German tourists discovered the body of a man frozen in a glacier in the Ötztal Alps, Italy. Tests showed that Ötzi, as scientists named him, had been preserved by the ice for 5,300 years, until the melting glacier ice revealed him.

Chemical analysis revealed that Ötzi's final meal was mountain goat

January 2002

March 2002

Collapsing ice shelves

In 2002, after several warm summers, the Larsen B ice shelf in Antarctica rapidly disintegrated. Satellite images showed 1,255 sq miles (3,250 sq km) of ice shattered into thousands of icebergs.

Thousands of icebergs, about to drift out into the ocean

Warming oceans

To date, the oceans have been warming up more slowly than the continents. The surface ocean warms first, and heat is eventually transferred to the deep oceans, which will continue warming even if greenhouse-gas emissions stop. Warming ocean water expands, and, together with melting ice on land, this is causing sea levels to rise.

Since the 1970s, the oceans have absorbed 90% of excess heat from CO$_2$ emissions.

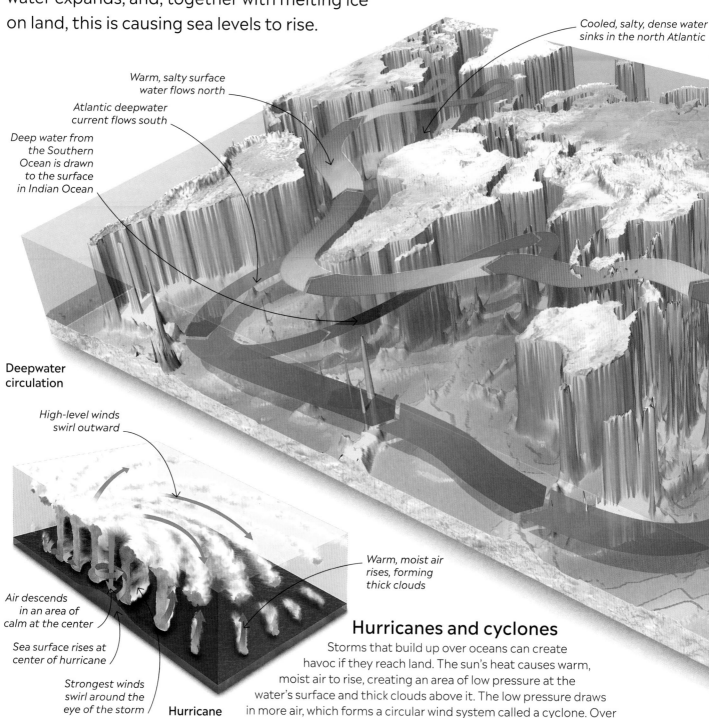

Cooled, salty, dense water sinks in the north Atlantic

Warm, salty surface water flows north

Atlantic deepwater current flows south

Deep water from the Southern Ocean is drawn to the surface in Indian Ocean

Deepwater circulation

High-level winds swirl outward

Warm, moist air rises, forming thick clouds

Air descends in an area of calm at the center

Sea surface rises at center of hurricane

Strongest winds swirl around the eye of the storm

Hurricane structure

Hurricanes and cyclones

Storms that build up over oceans can create havoc if they reach land. The sun's heat causes warm, moist air to rise, creating an area of low pressure at the water's surface and thick clouds above it. The low pressure draws in more air, which forms a circular wind system called a cyclone. Over tropical oceans, cyclones can develop into destructive hurricanes.

EYEWITNESS

Swamped cities

In March 2019, Cyclone Idai hit Mozambique. Gathering energy from increasingly warmer oceans, gusts of wind up to 143 mph (230 km/h) and extreme rainfall led to flash flooding and massive destruction of life and property.

Rising sea levels

As oceans warm up, they expand, so sea levels rise by a small amount. But gauges such as the one here in the North Sea show a far greater actual rise, indicating that melting ice is adding to the problem. Sea levels are predicted to keep rising for 1,000 years after all greenhouse-gas emissions stop—and for even longer if they don't.

Meltwater

Extra water making sea levels rise comes from melting glaciers (right) and continental ice sheets. If floating sea ice melts, it doesn't affect sea levels—the ice is already in the sea and simply changes from solid to liquid. But when ice on land melts, that water runs into the ocean.

CO_2 saturation

A quarter of the CO_2 in the air is absorbed by the oceans, where a lot of it is taken up by marine plankton. Warm oceans contain little plankton, so the CO_2 remains dissolved in the water. The stormy Southern Ocean (right) accounts for 15 percent of the CO_2 soaked up by oceans every year but may be so saturated that it cannot absorb any more.

Deep water is drawn to the surface in north Pacific Ocean

Warm surface current flows west across tropical Pacific Ocean

Cold, dense, deepwater current flows into Pacific Ocean

Current slowdown

Melting icebergs, glaciers, and permafrost add fresh water to the oceans, making them less salty, and this affects the mechanism that drives the deepwater currents. The north Atlantic deepwater flow could slow by up to half over the 21st century, disrupting the global circulation of water.

Flooded out

Rising sea levels are already flooding the coral islands of Tuvalu in the Pacific, where most of the land lies just 6–10 ft (2–3 m) above sea level. Higher tides make waves surge farther inland, swamping homes, farmland, and water supplies with salt water. Tuvalu's 11,000 citizens will gradually have to evacuate their islands, almost certainly forever.

31

Oceanic research

The dynamics of the ocean are a major part of the overall climate system. Every day, scientists work hard to gather data that enhance our understanding of the way the system works and how the oceans and atmosphere interact to influence climate change. Much of these data are obtained by sophisticated technology, including remote sensors on automated buoys, miniature submersibles, and satellites.

Satellite communications

Research ship

Meteorology platform

Launched in 2020, the British polar research ship RRS *Sir David Attenborough* is one of the most advanced research vessels used by scientists to study oceans and climate at first hand. It has enough fuel to stay at sea for up to 60 days, with 30 crew and 60 scientists. This ship is specifically designed to break though ice floes in the extreme environments of the polar oceans.

Navigation station

SIR DAVID ATTENBOROUGH

Bow designed to break through sea ice'

Remote-controlled AUV is 11.8 ft (3.6 m) long and can operate for up to 620 miles (1,000 km) or 20 days

Reef analysis

This diver is extracting a core sample from a Pacific coral island so that the growth of the coral reef can be analyzed. Patterns of coral growth over the centuries provide a valuable insight into the oceanic climates of the past, and they also mark fluctuations in sea level.

Beneath the waves

Boaty McBoatface is an unmanned submersible—an AUV (autonomous underwater vehicle). Carried on RRS *Sir David Attenborough*, it is designed to conduct research beneath floating sea ice in the Arctic and Antarctic oceans, reaching depths of 19,685 ft (6,000 m) under water.

Ocean ecology

Clouds of oceanic algae and other plankton absorb a lot of the CO_2 we pump into the atmosphere and turn it into food for other ocean life. Using satellite sensing, scientists monitor the global distribution of plankton and observe how it responds to climate change.

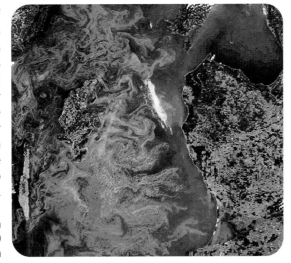

Satellite image of an algal bloom (in green) in the Baltic Sea

Data from the deep

Ocean currents have a powerful influence on climate because they redistribute heat around the globe. These sampling bottles gather water samples from different depths so that scientists can record their temperature and chemistry. This enables them to find out whether and how current patterns are changing.

Cabins

Laboratories and workshops

Main cargo crane

Winch system for lowering equipment overboard

Windspeed sensor

Air temperature sensor

Surface measurements

Understanding how the atmosphere and ocean interact is vital to the study of climates. Floating on the ocean surface, this research buoy is one of many that collect essential data, such as air and sea temperature, atmospheric pressure, and wind speed, and then transmit the data to a research base ship.

Acoustic probe

Oceanographers use sound signals to generate 3D maps of the ocean floor. Sound waves are also affected by water temperature, so they can be used to detect the flow of warm and cold water through the oceans and fluctuations that may be linked to global warming.

Living with
the heat

In the long term, wildlife evolves to cope with both cooler and warmer climates, but evolution is a harsh process. Many plants and animals cannot cope with the change and become extinct. Meanwhile, other organisms flourish because they adapt and develop features that enable them to survive. Recent wildlife losses may signal that we are at the beginning of a similar process now.

Out of step
Rising temperatures can disrupt the balance of nature. Europe's woodland caterpillars are hatching two weeks earlier in spring, so birds returning from Africa to breed arrive after most of the caterpillars have gone. They struggle to find food for their young.

Early losses
The golden toad discovered in the Monteverde forests of Costa Rica in 1966 was deemed extinct in 1991. The toads' young were attacked by a fungal disease that erupted as the nights became warmer. When the adult toads died, there were no young ones to take their place.

Starving seabirds
The oceanic food chain relies on the drifting plankton that fish feed on, which in turn feed predators such as seabirds. As warmer oceans alter the distribution of plankton, fish move away from seabird nesting sites. If this colony of guillemots cannot feed its young, it will fail.

Himalayan wildlife

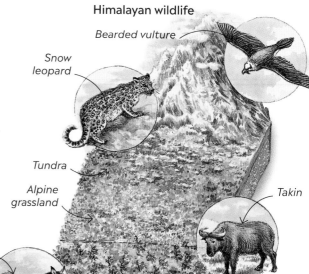

Bearded vulture

Snow leopard

Tundra

Alpine grassland

Asiatic ass

Cool coniferous forest

Hanuman langur

Subtropical deciduous forest

Takin

Low-growing shrubs

Red panda

Temperate deciduous forest

Uphill migrants
Many plants and animals are adapted for survival on high mountains where it is too cold for trees to grow. As temperatures rise, the trees creep uphill, forcing the mountain species uphill too. Eventually they may run out of space and become locally extinct.

Acidified oceans

When rain dissolves atmospheric carbon dioxide (CO_2), it forms a weak carbonic acid. The same process is affecting the oceans as they absorb extra CO_2 from the air, making them less alkaline. Many marine animals like this lobster need the alkaline minerals they absorb from seawater to build tough shells.

Powerful claw relies on strong shell

Malarial mosquitoes kill more than 400,000 people a year

On the move

Some animals may be adapting to climate change. Insects have short lifespans and breed rapidly, so they evolve quickly and move into new habitats. Disease-carrying mosquitoes are spreading malaria and West Nile virus to areas they once found too cold.

A diver observes bleached reefs in Moorea, French Polynesia, in 2019

Overheated reefs

Warming oceans bleach coral reefs, which turn white as they expel colorful microbes. These reefs—underwater rain forests—are home to an array of marine life. The stress from hot temperatures, along with bleaching, can cause them to die. Since 2016, nearly half of the corals on Australia's Great Barrier Reef have died from bleaching events.

Plight of the
polar bear

Climate change is a serious problem for the animals that hunt or breed on the sea ice of the Arctic. The ice is shrinking each year, and the summer ice may disappear altogether by 2070, or sooner. The most vulnerable of these animals is the species at the top of the food chain—the polar bear. If the ice vanishes, so, too, will the bear.

Shrinking ice

With rising temperatures, large areas of ocean once frozen year-round are now open water with a few scattered ice floes. Polar bears must swim long distances to find stable ice. The ice also melts earlier in summer, forcing the bears ashore—often before they have eaten enough to build up the thick fat reserves they need to survive until the sea freezes again.

A bleak future

If the Arctic sea ice disappears altogether in summer, the seals that polar bears prey upon will become scarce as they lose their icy breeding habitat. Female bears may not find enough food to see them through the winter when they nurse their young. If this happens, the polar bear will become extinct in the wild, with just a few surviving in zoos.

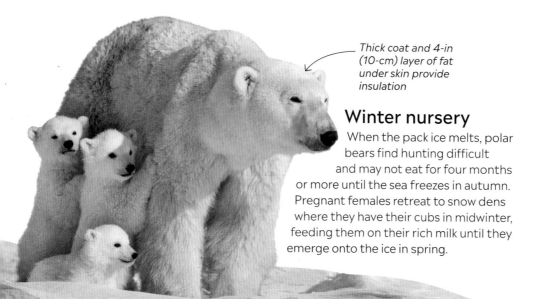

Thick coat and 4-in (10-cm) layer of fat under skin provide insulation

Winter nursery

When the pack ice melts, polar bears find hunting difficult and may not eat for four months or more until the sea freezes in autumn. Pregnant females retreat to snow dens where they have their cubs in midwinter, feeding them on their rich milk until they emerge onto the ice in spring.

Oceanic hunter

The polar bear catches ringed and bearded seals (its main prey) when they come up through holes in the sea ice to breathe. It detects these breathing holes by scent, from up to 0.6 mile (1 km) away. It also sniffs out the snow-covered ice caves of ringed seal pups and breaks through the ice to catch them.

Bearded seal

Scientists predict that polar bears could **become extinct** **due to global** **warming** **by the year 2100.**

Pollution and poisoning

Polar bears naturally eat a lot of fat to build up their own energy-rich fat reserves, and starving bears have been seen eating dumped industrial grease and even motor oil. Many bears are also becoming slowly poisoned through eating prey contaminated by pollution.

Sea bear

The polar bear lives on the pack ice on the surface of the Arctic Ocean but prefers the thinner yet stable ice that forms in winter around the fringes of the thick, permanent ice near the North Pole. It wanders over vast areas of the frozen ocean, but it can also swim for several hours to cross stretches of open water. In this way, it normally (they are moving into human communities for food) spends most of its life at sea.

EYEWITNESS

Conservation efforts
US Fish and Wildlife Service (FWS) researchers work on polar bear conservation. This includes managing human-polar bear conflicts with safety plans for bear encounters, using bear-proof food storage to reduce chances of bears entering human communities for food, and controlling bear hunting. Here, an FWS biologist monitors a tranquilized bear.

Climate models

How much warmer will it get, and how will that affect the world? There are a lot of factors to consider, so scientists build them into mathematical "models" of the climate, using computers to see what happens when the figures for greenhouse-gas emissions are increased. The projections demonstrate that if we don't do more to stop climate change, temperatures could rise by 5.4°F (3°C) or more by 2100—with potentially serious results.

Temperature and moisture exchange between the ocean and the atmosphere is a fundamental part of climate models

Land surfaces such as rain forests and deserts are shown

South America

Computer power

Computers forecast the changes in the atmosphere that control day-to-day weather, but forecasting long-term climate change is more difficult, with extra factors to consider, such as changes in vegetation and ice cover. But supercomputers can process vast amounts of data, and every year they become more powerful and, crucially, help scientists' understanding of the changing climate.

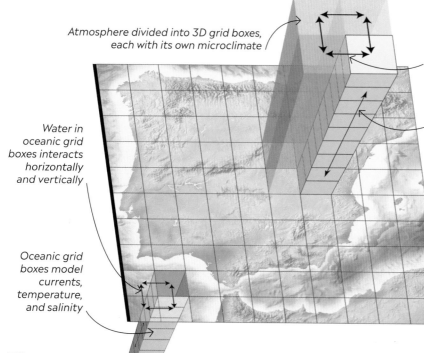

Atmosphere divided into 3D grid boxes, each with its own microclimate

Air in grid boxes interacts horizontally

Air in grid boxes interacts vertically

Water in oceanic grid boxes interacts horizontally and vertically

Oceanic grid boxes model currents, temperature, and salinity

Climate modeling

A climate model is a computerized representation of the atmosphere based on a three-dimensional global grid. This is linked to submodels of other global systems, such as the oceans, as shown here, or vegetation. The computer program allows some factors to be changed, such as the amount of CO_2 in the atmosphere. The model then applies these changes to its virtual world to see what effect they have on climate.

Running the model

When it is run on the computer, a climate model evolves in a series of short time steps, often of less than an hour each, and each step may take a few seconds to process. Achieving a projection to the end of the century takes several weeks, even on a powerful supercomputer. The results can then be used to generate graphs and images that show how temperatures and rainfall might change in different circumstances. This image has been generated from a model of changing global sea temperatures.

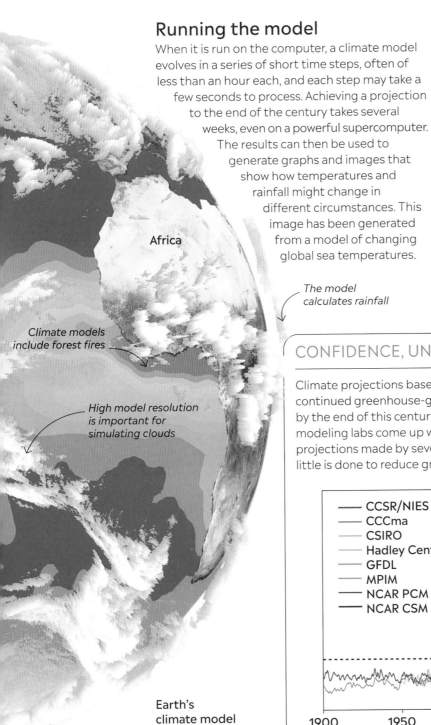

Africa

The model calculates rainfall

Climate models include forest fires

High model resolution is important for simulating clouds

Earth's climate model

EYEWITNESS

Syukuro Manabe

Japanese meteorologist Syukuro Manabe helped develop the first global climate model by using computers in 1967. This predicted that increasing CO_2 levels would cause a rise in Earth's temperature.

CONFIDENCE, UNCERTAINTY

Climate projections based on long-term global averages show that continued greenhouse-gas emissions will lead to higher temperatures by the end of this century. But with so many variables, different modeling labs come up with different projections. This graph shows projections made by seven labs, using the same basic scenario that little is done to reduce greenhouse-gas emissions.

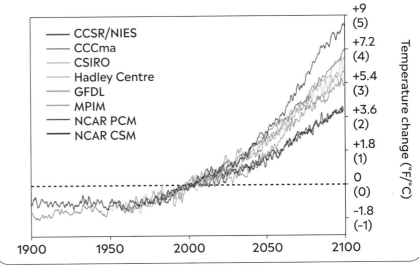

- CCSR/NIES
- CCCma
- CSIRO
- Hadley Centre
- GFDL
- MPIM
- NCAR PCM
- NCAR CSM

Temperature change (°F/°C)

+9 (5)
+7.2 (4)
+5.4 (3)
+3.6 (2)
+1.8 (1)
0 (0)
−1.8 (−1)

1900   1950   2000   2050   2100

DIFFERENT SCENARIOS

Climate models use different "scenarios." These cover the various ways in which the world might develop. The basic scenario assumes steady economic growth and a corresponding increase in greenhouse-gas emissions. Others might include a major switch away from them. These globes show predicted temperature rises by 2099 based on two scenarios: a low-emission scenario (1) and a high-emission scenario (2).

Scenario 1

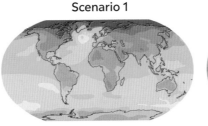

Scenario 2

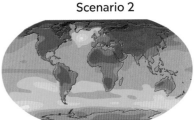

Temperature change (°C)

0.0 0.5 1.0 1.5 2.0 2.5 3.0 3.5 4.0 4.5 5.0 5.5 6.0 6.5

This century

The global average temperature is certain to rise in the 21st century. Even if we stopped adding greenhouse gases to the atmosphere, the heat stored in the oceans would continue to be released over several decades. This will lead to frequent and extreme heatwaves, droughts, and floods; rising sea levels; and the extinction of threatened species. Some of this is inevitable, but if we try to combat climate change, we will be able to limit the damage.

Shifting vegetation zones

As the polar regions warm up and the subtropics turn to deserts, wild plants will creep toward the poles. Evergreen trees like these pines will move into treeless Arctic tundra, and in warmer, drier areas, grass will take over from woodland. But if vast tracts of farmland disrupt this natural migration, many species will die out.

Expanding deserts

Rainfall is predicted to decrease in subtropical lands, and many are already semideserts. Drylands will increase by 11–23 percent, spreading into neighboring scrubland, grassland, and farmland. Farther north and south, summer heatwaves are likely to become more frequent and extreme.

The Pudong district of Shanghai

THE NORTH POLE

These images show the extent of Arctic summer ice in 1985 and its projected extent in 2085. The loss of ice will be a catastrophe for the ice-breeding seals and polar bears in the region. Increased meltwater from Greenland into the sea may also affect the currents that influence oceanic food chains and global weather systems.

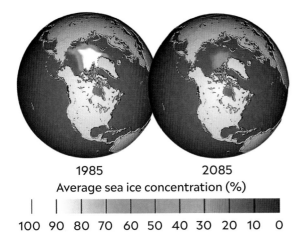

1985   2085

Average sea ice concentration (%)

| 100 | 90 | 80 | 70 | 60 | 50 | 40 | 30 | 20 | 10 | 0 |

Storm warning

In 2017, Hurricane Harvey devastated Texas. In parts of the state, the intense storm brought historic levels of rainfall—up to 60.58 in (1,539 mm) in four days. With more than 20 trillion gallons (76 trillion liters) of water dumped on southeast Texas, a combination of rainfall and the tide caused flooding of up to 10 ft (3 m).

Wildlife extinctions

If the average global temperature continues to rise, 15 to 37 percent of wildlife species, such as this rare orchid, could be extinct by 2050. However, more adaptable species, including rats, may flourish.

Vulnerable cities

Sea levels will keep rising as more glacial meltwater pours into the oceans. By the year 2100, it is likely to be 17–33 in (43–84 cm) higher than it is now, provided nothing catastrophic happens to the great continental ice sheets of Greenland or Antarctica. Cities on low-lying coasts are at risk from flooding.

Shanghai in China is only
10-16 ft (3-5 m)
above sea level.

What scares
the scientists?

Unless we increase our efforts to combat climate change, global temperatures could rise high enough to trigger events like the mass melting of Arctic permafrost or huge wildfires in Amazonia. These would release more greenhouse gases, such as carbon dioxide (CO_2) and methane, accelerating global warming. We know that catastrophic climate change has happened in the distant past. To stop it from happening again, we must act now.

Burning rain forests

As temperatures rise, rain forests are drying out and burning or dying from drought. Trees pump water into the air through their leaves, so fewer trees mean less rain. This process could destroy Earth's richest ecosystem, and as the trees burn or decay, all the carbon in their timber will turn to CO_2, raising temperatures still further.

Acid oceans

As oceans get warmer and become more acidic through absorbing CO_2, many marine organisms will start to die off. If temperatures rise to 3.6°F (2°C) above pre-industrial levels, up to 97 percent of the world's coral reefs could suffer "coral bleaching" and die. In acidified water, organisms such as crabs, clams, and microscopic plankton can't build their shells. If their numbers dwindle, so will the fish that feed on them, which could lead to a mass extinction involving many types of marine life.

Massive sea-level rise

Most scientists think that sea levels will rise by 39 in (1 m) by 2100. But if the immensely thick ice sheets of Antarctica and Greenland start to collapse in a big way, sea levels could eventually rise by up to 82 ft (25 m). Even a 23-ft (7-m) rise —the effect of the Greenland ice sheet collapsing—would swamp coastal cities, such as London, New York, Tokyo, Shanghai, and Calcutta.

Houses in Bangladesh have already been lost to rising sea level

Melting the tundra

In the far north, when the permafrost partly thaws in the summer, huge swamps full of decaying vegetation release methane. As rising temperatures cause more permafrost melt each summer, more methane will be released, adding to the greenhouse effect.

Ice lost at the fringes increases the flow of ice toward the ocean

Collapsing ice sheets

The fringes of the Greenland and west Antarctic ice sheets are melting faster than ever recorded before, with huge slabs of ice breaking off and floating away as icebergs. This could cause the ice sheets to collapse, making sea levels rise dramatically.

Frozen methane

Methane from decaying organic material on the seafloor is usually frozen. If the water temperature rises, it will melt, releasing methane. It will take centuries for ocean depths to get warm enough for this to happen, but this may have contributed to extreme global warming in the past.

Mass extinction

About 250 million years ago, 96 percent of all species died out when a colossal amount of CO_2 release by massive volcanic activity raised the average temperature by 10.8–14.4°F (6–8°C). Global temperatures could plausibly increase by 7.2°F (4°C) by 2100—and possibly more.

Who is most vulnerable?

Climate change will have a big impact on human society. The people who are likely to suffer most are those who have done least to create the problem—those who live in the developing world. Many already have to cope with extreme climates. Climate change will likely bring more famines, mass migrations, and conflicts over land and resources. Industrialized societies will suffer too, both directly and because of serious problems in other parts of the world.

Rising waters

Many highly populated coastal parts of the world lie close to sea level. They include the Ganges Delta region of India and Bangladesh. If a hurricane caused catastrophic flooding on top of this, it would have disastrous results.

Disease

As the world warms up, tropical diseases appear to be spreading. Malaria, which is carried by tropical mosquitoes, infected around 230 million people worldwide in 2018. Blood tests will reveal whether this child has also been infected.

Farm crops

In temperate regions, cereal crops such as wheat may benefit from the longer summers. However, global warming could make farming harder in tropical countries. Many crops are grown in regions that could become too warm for the plants to survive.

A projected sea level rise of about 20 in (50 cm) in Bangladesh could **displace 15 million people by 2050.**

Survivors of a flood in 2020 row through flooded areas on a makeshift raft in Assam, India

People on the move

Failed harvests caused by drought are resulting in mass migration from Central American countries, such as Honduras (pictured), El Salvador, and Guatemala. The World Bank estimates that around 2 million people from Central America will become climate change refugees by 2050.

Water resources

Clean, fresh water is vital to life, but droughts will make it scarce in areas that are already semideserts. Shrinking glaciers could have the same effect. For example, large areas of central Asia and China rely on water stored in the glaciers of the Himalayas—if the glaciers melt, the water they contain will drain away. Flooding by rising sea levels could also contaminate water supplies for cities built on low-lying coasts.

Infrastructure breakdown

Developed countries rely on a network of services, such as power, communications, and transportation, to provide the necessities of life, including food, water, and heating. This makes them just as vulnerable to destructive events as less complex societies, as the US discovered when Hurricane Katrina hit New Orleans in 2005.

Food supply

If farming in the tropics is badly hurt by climate change, food supplies could suffer. The worst hit will be people in developing countries who already struggle to get enough to eat. Food grown in the tropics is eaten all over the world, so developed nations will also be affected.

Adapting to
climate change

Even if we stopped all greenhouse-gas emissions tomorrow, the average global temperature would still keep rising for the next 30 years, due mainly to the gradual release of heat stored by the oceans. Rising temperatures are likely to raise sea levels, cause more droughts and floods, and damage agriculture and wildlife. So we must prepare for these changes while working to stop the problem from getting worse.

Tidal defenses

Many great cities are built on low-lying coasts vulnerable to rising sea levels. Most of these cities already have sea defenses but will need extra protection against extra-high tides and storm surges. In the UK, the Thames Barrier was built in 1974–1982 to protect London from storm surges at sea that were already seen as a threat.

Lifting mechanism to close each gate

Soaking up storms

Concrete city streets can't absorb heavy rain, creating blocked drains and floods of stormwater and sewage. Green spaces like Central Park in New York soak up rainwater and help avoid such flooding.

Natural barriers

The sea naturally builds up shingle banks, salt marshes, and mangrove swamps. Preserving these important habitats from destruction by coastal development can help protect coasts from flooding.

Wildlife reserves

Habitat destruction and the stress of changing climates will drive many species into extinction. Nature reserves protect wildlife, aid research, and house the ecosystems that resist climate change.

Safe refuges

In flat, low-lying Bangladesh, the Ganges and other rivers burst their banks after heavy monsoon rains, so people build large mounds as a refuge for their families and cattle. When the floods drain away, they can move back onto the surrounding land.

Island of silt

The Thames Barrier could prevent flooding until 2060-2070.

Circular steel gate is 66 ft (20 m) high

Nine of these piers and 10 steel gates cover the 1,700-ft (520-m) width of the river

Battling the deserts

People living on the fringes of expanding deserts can stop the sand from taking over by planting barriers of drought-resistant grasses and shrubs to stabilize the dunes. They can also keep dry grasslands from turning into desert by preventing farm animals from overgrazing.

👁 EYEWITNESS

New farm crops
The International Rice Research Institute (IRRI) is developing new rice plants that will grow in severe conditions, such as droughts and floods brought on by climate change. Drought-tolerant rice varieties by IRRI are now grown in India, Nepal, and the Philippines.

Combating
climate change

Climate change is a global problem that requires a global response, but getting all the nations to agree on solutions is difficult. Replacing the technologies that are causing the problem is costly, but we have more to lose by risking climate chaos. By degrees, agreements are being forged to combat climate change.

The Paris Agreement

In 2015, at a United Nations summit in Paris, 195 countries reached an agreement to intensify efforts to combat climate change. Central to the agreement was a target of limiting global temperature rise to less than 3.6°F (2°C).

An equal share

As developing countries with low emissions, such as Peru, push for better living standards, their greenhouse-gas emissions will increase. It is not fair to expect them to sacrifice this development. To compensate, rich nations that have emitted large quantities of greenhouse gases for years need to make greater reductions.

👁 EYEWITNESS

Greta Thunberg
Born in 2003, Swedish climate activist Greta Thunberg began her school strike for the climate in 2018, inspiring many more around the globe. In 2019, she addressed the UN Climate Action Summit and criticized world leaders: "Entire ecosystems are collapsing. We are in the beginning of a mass extinction, and all you can talk about is money and fairy tales of eternal economic growth. How dare you!"

2019 climate strike

A growing number of young people across the world are protesting for greater action against climate change from governments. In September 2019, 7.6 million people took part in a global climate strike.

Climate strike in Bangkok, Thailand

THE TARGET

To limit global warming below 2.7°F (2°C) or ideally 3.6°F (1.5°C), as set out in the Paris Agreement, emissions of greenhouse gases need to be reduced quickly. This graph shows that governments need more ambitious policies to cut their emissions to reach these temperature targets.

- ● Current policies
- ● 3.6°F (2°C) target
- ● 2.7°F (1.5°C) target

Gt = gigaton

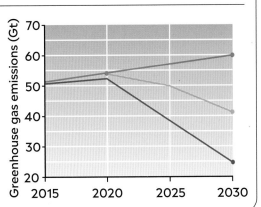

Carbon trading

Under international agreements to reduce greenhouse-gas emissions, countries that cannot meet their targets have to buy "carbon credits" from nations with very low carbon emissions. The total emissions of both nations cannot exceed their combined quotas. High-carbon nations can also fund projects in low-carbon nations, such as restoring forests by using native trees like this teak seedling.

Clean energy

Nations around the world are using more renewable energy. Danish energy company Ørsted was named the world's most sustainable company in 2020 after it shut down coal power plants and replaced them with sources of renewable energy, such as wind farms.

The IPCC

In 1988, the United Nations asked for a high-level scientific assessment of the evidence for climate change. This led to the creation of the Intergovernmental Panel on Climate Change, or IPCC. Its role is to look at all the climate research carried out worldwide and produce regular, detailed assessments of the scientists' conclusions. The first of these assessment reports was released in 1990, and it was followed by updated reports in 1995, 2001, 2007, and 2014.

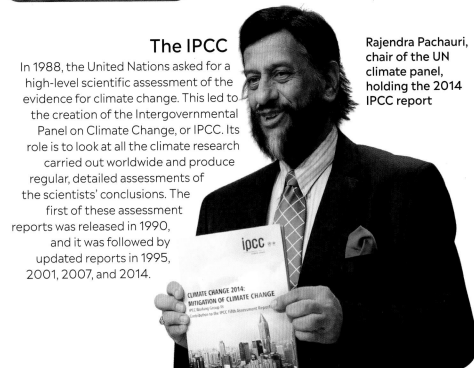

Rajendra Pachauri, chair of the UN climate panel, holding the 2014 IPCC report

Cutting
the carbon

Currently, the world relies on electricity from fossil fuels, but this must be replaced by renewable forms of energy. Countries around the world are now trying to reduce the amount of fossil fuels they use and also increase the amount of CO_2 they remove from the atmosphere by planting trees.

Decline of coal

Coal is the dirtiest fossil fuel, and the one that fueled the Industrial Revolution. Some industrialized nations are now making large reductions to the amount of coal they use. In 2019, for example, the UK used the lowest amount of coal in 250 years.

Coal-burning power station in the Netherlands

Natural gas

Burning natural gas instead of coal to generate power releases less CO_2, but gas is a fossil fuel and releases CO_2 into the atmosphere. Gas is not a solution to climate change and needs to be replaced by renewable energy, such as wind and solar.

Many forest trees have been cut down to make way for this gas pipeline in Alaska

The price of coal

Reducing consumption of coal has other benefits, as coal mining is dangerous and often destructive. Deep coal mines are notorious for deadly tunnel collapses, flooding, fires, and explosions. In 2006, when this photograph was taken in Sichuan, China, at least 5,986 Chinese workers were killed in mining accidents. Surface mines are safer, but they leave huge scars on the landscape.

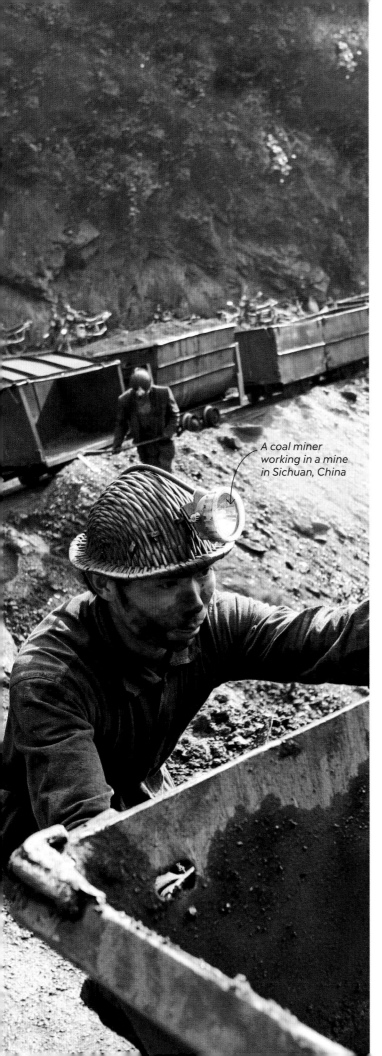

A coal miner working in a mine in Sichuan, China

Reaching Net Zero

National governments support cutting carbon by making "Net Zero" targets meaning that a nation is not emitting a greater amount of greenhouse gases into the atmosphere than it is removing from the atmosphere. To stop global warming, global emissions need to reach Net Zero. Many nations have Net Zero deadlines of 2050, but Sweden has signed a more ambitious target of 2045, set by politician Isabella Lövin.

Isabella Lövin cycling to the People's Climate March, 2018

98% of electricity in Costa Rica comes from
carbon-free sources.

Planting trees

One way to reach Net Zero sooner is to increase how much CO_2 is absorbed from the atmosphere by carbon sinks. The most effective way of doing this is to restore Earth's forests by planting trees. Around the world, governments are launching tree-planting programs. The Bonn Challenge is a global campaign that aims to restore 865 million acres (350 million ha) of deforested landscapes by 2030.

Nuclear **power**

There is one powerful, reliable energy source that emits no greenhouse gases. Nuclear fission exploits the colossal amount of energy released by radioactive uranium when its atoms are split in a nuclear reactor. But radiation is extremely dangerous, and because a reactor can also be used to make nuclear weapons, nuclear power is the subject of fierce debate between those who support this form of energy generation and those who oppose it.

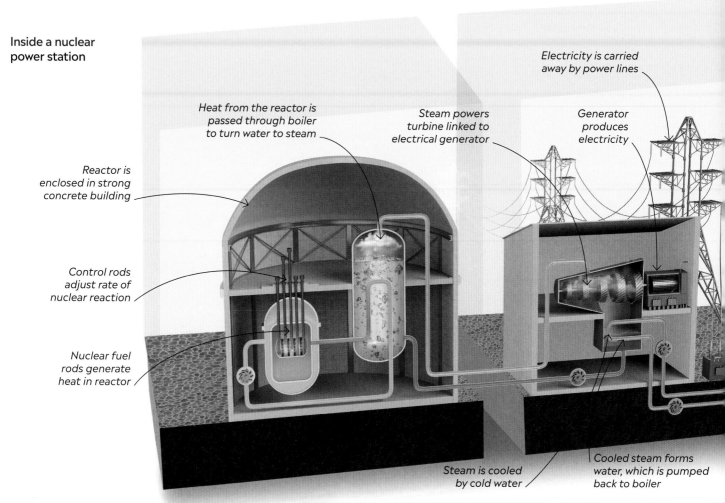

Inside a nuclear power station

Heat from the reactor is passed through boiler to turn water to steam

Steam powers turbine linked to electrical generator

Electricity is carried away by power lines

Generator produces electricity

Reactor is enclosed in strong concrete building

Control rods adjust rate of nuclear reaction

Nuclear fuel rods generate heat in reactor

Steam is cooled by cold water

Cooled steam forms water, which is pumped back to boiler

Nuclear power station

A nuclear power station's reactor contains rods of radioactive uranium that interact in a nuclear chain reaction. The reaction is regulated by control rods that are lowered between the radioactive fuel rods to absorb neutrons and prevent the rods' interaction. The heat generated by the reaction heats liquid that is pumped through a boiler to turn water into steam. This powers turbines linked to electricity generators.

FISSION

A single atom of uranium can be made to yield a huge amount of energy by hitting it with a tiny particle called a neutron. This splits the nucleus at its heart in two, releasing energy and more neutrons. These split more nuclei in a chain reaction. If this is not controlled, it can cause a nuclear explosion, but if it takes place in a nuclear reactor, it simply generates a lot of heat.

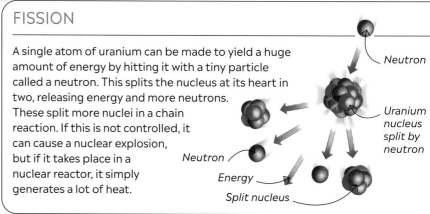

Neutron

Uranium nucleus split by neutron

Neutron

Energy

Split nucleus

A cooling tower circulates water in a closed-loop steam cycle and releases excess heat into the air

Hot water flows to cooling tower

Cooled water returns from cooling tower

FUSION

Atomic nuclei smashed together can fuse to make bigger nuclei, producing huge amounts of energy. This does not involve radioactive fuel or radioactive waste, but it takes a huge input of energy to get started, and controlling it is very difficult.

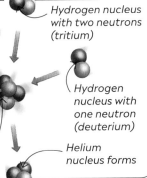

Hydrogen nucleus with two neutrons (tritium)

Neutron released

Hydrogen nucleus with one neutron (deuterium)

Nuclei collide and fuse

Helium nucleus forms

Nuclear weapons
With expertise in nuclear technology comes the risk that countries may develop highly dangerous nuclear weapons, including nuclear bombs, and threaten international stability.

Carbon-free power
More than 70 percent of France's electricity is generated by nuclear energy. It powers TGV trains that cover long distances at up to 186 mph (300 km/h), rivaling aircraft for speed but with zero carbon emissions. Many nations would like to follow France's example, but nuclear power stations are very expensive and take a long time to build.

Uranium mining
Uranium—the radioactive metal used as nuclear fuel—is a rare metal that may be in short supply within a few decades. Uranium mining uses a lot of conventional energy that generates greenhouse gases, as does the construction of a nuclear power station, so nuclear power is not entirely carbon-neutral. Mining also leaves huge scars in the landscape.

Radioactive waste
A nuclear power station uses a tiny quantity of nuclear fuel, which then remains highly radioactive for thousands of years. The radiation is very dangerous to health. The waste must be stored in special facilities while scientists try to find ways to make it safe. Here, used nuclear fuel is stored in a tank of water, which stops the radiation from escaping.

Fusion experiment
Scientists from 35 nations are building the world's first power station to use nuclear fusion. The International Thermonuclear Experimental Reactor (ITER) in France will help develop a new way of producing low-carbon electricity.

Renewable energy

For centuries, people have harnessed the energy of wind and flowing water to power windmills and water mills—and now to drive electricity generators. Solar and geothermal energy can also be turned into electricity. Unlike fossil fuels, these energy sources are "renewable"—they never run out. Technologies such as solar and wind farms do not release the greenhouse gases that are causing climate change.

Hydroelectric power

Rivers can be used to power turbines linked to electricity generators. To ensure a steady flow, huge dams hold the water in reservoirs. Hydroelectric power supplies 16 percent of the world's electricity.

Geothermal energy

In volcanic regions, energy tapped from hot rock and water beneath the ground can be used to heat water and houses and to run the turbines of power stations like this one at Wairakei, New Zealand.

Wind farms

Wind is being harnessed on a large scale by wind farms of high-tech turbines. Many are on land, but offshore sites like this one near Copenhagen, Denmark, get stronger, more consistent winds.

Solar power plants

The most common form of solar power uses panels with cells that can produce electricity directly from sunlight. But there are also systems that use mirrors to focus the sun's rays onto a tower that collects the heat and uses it to run a turbine and generator.

WATER PRESSURE

A hydroelectric scheme relies on the immense water pressure created by having a colossal weight of water trapped behind the dam. The water pressure spins the blades of several huge turbines built into tunnels in the dam, and these turbines turn the generators that produce electricity. The water flow is controlled by sluice gates in the tunnels, so the output of the power plant can be matched to supply water on demand.

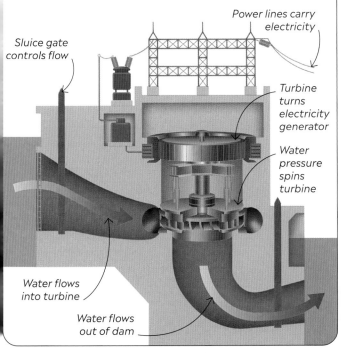

Power lines carry electricity

Sluice gate controls flow

Turbine turns electricity generator

Water pressure spins turbine

Water flows into turbine

Water flows out of dam

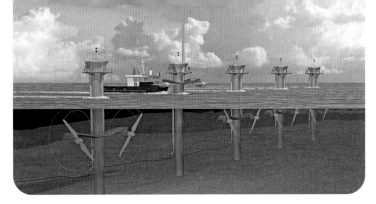

Waves and ocean currents

Power plants that harness wave energy work well only on exposed sites that can rely on big waves year-round. One day, giant submarine turbines might be used to generate power from ocean currents, which are always fast-flowing. Schemes like this could produce as much electricity as a nuclear power plant.

Biofuel crops

Burning a plant product as fuel releases carbon dioxide, but new crops can then be planted to absorb this gas. However, growing biofuel crops such as sugar cane often uses land needed for food crops or cleared by deforestation. It also generates greenhouse gases through the use of fertilizers and machinery.

Cut sugar cane

Ivanpah Solar Electric Generating System in Mojave Desert

Power for the people

Big power plants generating electricity are essential for keeping large-scale infrastructure running, but households and small communities can provide some or even all of their own power without using fossil fuels. Some is in the form of electricity, and some is in the form of heat energy. The more people switch to devices such as solar panels and heat pumps, the less expensive this technology will become.

Solar hot water

Solar energy is free, abundant, and nonpolluting. Many systems use roof panels made of copper pipes in glass tubes. Sunlight passing through the glass heats fluid pumped through the pipes, and the hot fluid heats the water used for bathing and washing.

Wood-burning stoves

Burning wood or similar plant products in a solid-fuel stove to provide heat can be carbon-neutral, if the amount of CO_2 it releases is absorbed by the growth of new fuel plants. But such biomass fuels are only suitable for small-scale use. Growing enough fuel to power a city would require too much land.

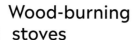

Solar electricity

Solar panels are used to generate electricity. These are built up from many solar photovoltaic elements that convert light into electrical energy. They work best in sunny places and can run air-conditioning systems that use the most power when the sun is shining. In the developing world, solar panels linked to batteries provide lighting for homes. Here, the clear skies over Central Asia allow a small solar array to power the satellite belonging to a Mongolian family.

Photovoltaic solar panel

Satellite dish, a link to the outside world

GROUND-SOURCE HEAT PUMPS

In winter, the temperature below ground stays higher than the air above. The heat can be collected by using a long, buried coil of pipe containing water and antifreeze, and the warmed fluid is pumped through a heat-exchanger linked to an underfloor heating system.

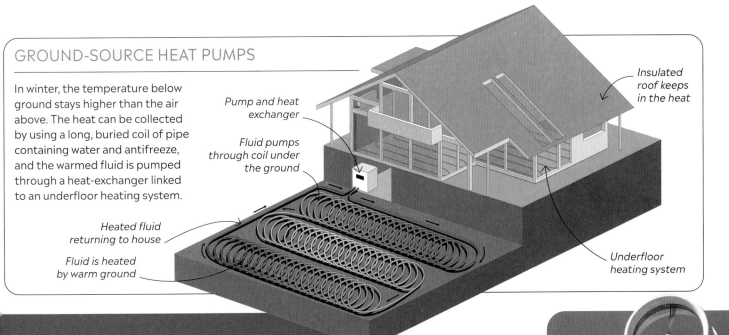

Pump and heat exchanger

Fluid pumps through coil under the ground

Insulated roof keeps in the heat

Heated fluid returning to house

Fluid is heated by warm ground

Underfloor heating system

Every hour, the sun radiates more than enough energy to meet Earth's global needs for an entire year.

Wind turbines

A small wind turbine such as this one generates only a small fraction of the electricity used by a typical household. Turbines will become more efficient, and, if people find ways of using less energy, local or domestic wind power will become a more viable option.

Home hydro

Harnessing the power of a fast-flowing stream close by can provide free, reliable electricity without generating any greenhouse gases. These small hydroelectric systems use small turbines, but they require a good head of water to build up enough water pressure and keep the turbine running during dry weather.

Simple technology

Wind pumps have been used to pump water for centuries. Small power generators are more complex, but many can still be maintained by the people who use them. This makes them ideal for use in developing countries and in remote communities far from national grid networks.

Energy
efficiency

Supplying power without using the fossil fuels that contribute to climate change is a challenge. If we all used energy more efficiently, there would be less demand. As a result renewable energy sources, such as wind and solar power, would account for a greater proportion, and the need for fossil fuels would decrease.

Many homes generate electricity from rooftop solar panels

Building standards

This infrared image shows heat escaping from a house as red and white, while cooler (insulated) areas are blue. In Sweden, new houses that meet strict building standards lose less heat, reducing the need for central heating and using four times less energy than many older houses in the UK.

Efficiency rating label

Energy rating

Some home equipment, such as fridges, must be left on all the time, and others, such as washing machines, may run for hours each day, using a lot of water and wasting a lot of energy if they work inefficiently. To encourage the purchase of energy-efficient designs, labels on new appliances show their energy consumption and their water consumption.

Efficient lighting

Incandescent bulbs are highly inefficient. About 5 percent of the electricity used to power a standard 100-watt light bulb is converted into light—the other 95 percent is wasted as heat. Compact fluorescent energy-saving bulbs produce about four times as much light per watt of electricity. Bulbs that use clusters of light-emitting diodes (LEDs) are even more efficient and last longer.

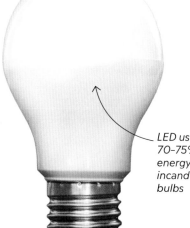

LED uses 70–75% less energy than incandescent bulbs

Friebürg aims to use
100% renewable
energy by 2035.

Shops and offices

Vast amounts of energy are wasted in shops and offices. Big food stores have rows of open fridges spilling out cold air. Office air conditioning, lights, and computers are often left on at night. By contrast, the Swiss Re Tower in London in the UK is designed to save energy. Its shape minimizes the cooling effects of the wind and maximizes natural light, reducing the use of heating and lighting.

👁 EYEWITNESS

A green city
Urban areas can be designed to reduce their impact on the climate. Freiburg in Germany (pictured) is an example of a successful eco-city, where the majority of electricity comes from renewable sources. Cars are banned from the city center, replaced by cycling and public transportation.

Eco-homes

Some homes are designed to have a low environmental impact. The homes shown here, in Freiburg, Germany, obtain energy from renewable sources, such as solar panels on the roof. Wall and roof insulation ensure they are warm in the winter and cool in the summer.

Wasteful design

Even if it is not in use, a device plugged into a power socket still uses power unless the power supply is switched off at the wall. Gadgets with built-in clocks and tuners have to be left on standby all the time. Plasma-screen TVs use almost five times more energy than smaller traditional TVs and 30–65 percent more energy than equally big LCD models.

Green transport

The transportation of people and freight accounts for at least 16 percent of global greenhouse-gas emissions, but that figure is rising. Technology may help with the development of more efficient vehicles, powered by less polluting fuels. But for now, the best way to reduce these emissions from transportation is to change the way we travel and to travel less.

Public transportation

Public transportation systems are more energy-efficient than cars because they carry a lot of passengers and often use more energy-saving technology, such as electric power. Away from urban centers, there are fewer buses and trains, so many people use cars. But if rising fuel prices and road congestion encourage more people to use public transportation, services may improve as a result.

Pedal power

Over short distances, bikes are quicker than cars. Beijing in China is famous for its crowds of cyclists. Many other cities also encourage cycling, and cars are banned from some city centers. The result is a much cleaner, safer, friendlier environment, with far fewer greenhouse-gas emissions.

Electric trains

Electric trains emit 20–35% less carbon than diesel trains per passenger per mile. They are also faster, have lower fuel costs, and reduce air pollution. They are far more efficient than road transportation and aviation.

Lightweight materials reduce emissions

Electric cars

Many vehicle manufacturers have started producing fully electric cars, such as this Tesla Model S. Powered by only an electric motor connected to a battery, it does not produce any emissions when driven.

Hydrogen

Scientists are experimenting with ways to use hydrogen gas to power vehicles. Large amounts of hydrogen can be compressed into fuel cells (seen here on the bus roof), which are used to power electric motors. The only emission from hydrogen-fueled engines is water vapor.

Biofuels

Biofuels are made from organic plant matter, such as oil palm (shown here), corn, soy, and sugarcane. They are blended with gas and diesel to reduce emissions. However, deforesting land to grow biofuel crops means that this fuel has limited benefits.

HYBRID CARS

Hybrid cars are powered by both a gas engine and an electric motor. For short journeys at low speeds, the car uses the electric motor fueled by a battery, with no emissions. At high speeds and over longer distances, the gas engine powers the car and charges the battery. Hybrid cars can reduce emissions but also work where charging stations are generally unavailable.

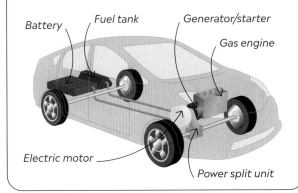

Battery   *Fuel tank*   *Generator/starter*   *Gas engine*
Electric motor   *Power split unit*

Recycled fuels

Growing crops to make biofuels can do more harm than good, but diesel engines can be modified to use cleaned, recycled cooking oil and oils from other waste products. Many countries, including the UK, are looking to reduce their emissions by powering buses with recycled biofuels.

Charging point

Strong frame forms safety cage

To stay powered, the battery must be regularly connected to an electric charging station

Your carbon footprint

You can help halt climate change by reducing your carbon footprint—the amount of greenhouse gases, including carbon dioxide (CO_2), released as a result of the things you do. Every one of us can make more climate-friendly lifestyle choices, such as thinking about what we eat, buying less, reusing and recycling more, and using low-emission transportation.

Use your legs

Cars are responsible for a lot of our greenhouse-gas emissions, so try to use them less—especially for short journeys, which use far more fuel per mile than long ones. Use public transportation if you can, or, if the roads are safe, walk or cycle—it will also get you in shape! If a car is the only option, share a ride or get a lift with friends.

Eat less meat

Raising animals—in particular cattle—adds methane to the atmosphere. Rain forests are also cleared to provide grazing for beef cattle. Importing meat from abroad uses fossil fuels and increases emissions. Every mouthful of beef we eat may involve the emission of up to 6,800 times its own weight in greenhouse gases.

 EYEWITNESS

Reforestation in Ethiopia

In 2019, Ethiopians planted four billion seedlings as part of its five-year "Green Legacy" plan to tackle deforestation. This national campaign aims to plant 20 billion trees by 2024 to combat desertification and absorb CO_2.

Turn it down

A thermostat switches heat off when the room warms up. Setting it just 1.8°F (1°C) lower saves 518 lb (235 kg) of CO_2 emissions per year. Aim for 61–64°F (16–18°C); if you are a bit cold, wear more clothes.

Take the train

Avoid short flights. A flight from London to Paris releases 538 lb (244 kg) of CO_2 per passenger, but a high-speed train releases 48 lb (22 kg) per passenger. For long-haul flights, look into carbon-offsetting options, which balance the plane's emissions by cutting greenhouse gases elsewhere.

Buy local

Shop locally, and on foot or by bus rather than by car. Try to avoid buying foods from halfway around the globe. Check the country of origin labels, cut back to just the occasional exotic treat, and look for other options from local sources. And try not to buy things that come with a lot of packaging.

Switch it off

Huge amounts of greenhouse gas are created by leaving electronic equipment switched on for no reason. Even standby mode still uses power, as do chargers when left plugged in. If you can switch off unused equipment at the wall without affecting the data stored in its memory, then do it.

Recycling bins take all kinds of waste

Cans & Bottles

PET Bottles

Others

Reuse and recycle

Throwing things away contributes to climate change by adding to methane-generating landfills and encouraging us to buy new things whose manufacture emits greenhouse gases. Use things for as long as possible. If they cannot be repaired, try to recycle them.

63

Greenhouse-gas producers

Climate change is being caused by humans adding greenhouse gases such as carbon dioxide (CO_2) to the atmosphere in various ways. Some nations release a lot more than others, partly because they are larger, but also because most of their citizens are richer and have a bigger carbon footprint.

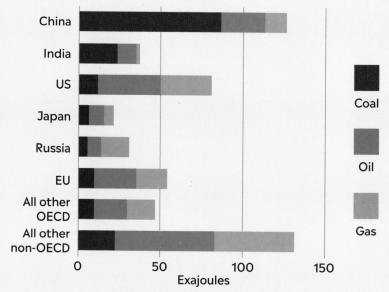

Electricity and heat 30.4%

Transport 15.9%

Waste and other 4.8%

Buildings 5.5%

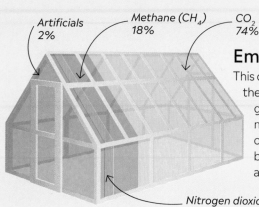

Artificials 2%

Methane (CH_4) 18%

CO_2 74%

Emissions by weight

This diagram shows the relative quantities of the major human-produced greenhouse gases. The most important is CO_2, as so much of it is released every year. The others are emitted in smaller quantities, but they have a big effect because they are more powerful than CO_2.

Nitrogen dioxide (NO_2) 6%

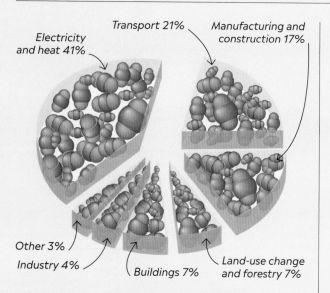

Electricity and heat 41%

Transport 21%

Manufacturing and construction 17%

Other 3%

Industry 4%

Buildings 7%

Land-use change and forestry 7%

Carbon dioxide by sector

Of all the greenhouse gases, CO_2 currently has the most impact on the climate. Most of it is being emitted from power plants that burn coal or natural gas, but a lot is released by industry and transportation. The land-use sector includes the felling and burning of forests.

China

India

US

Japan

Russia

EU

All other OECD

All other non-OECD

0   50   100   150
Exajoules

Coal

Oil

Gas

Fossil-fuel consumption

The main source of CO_2 is the burning of fossil fuels. The biggest consumers of fossil fuels are China, the United States, and the European Union. Coal produces far more CO_2 per unit of energy than other fuels, so countries that burn a lot of coal, such as China, have a bigger impact on the climate than countries that burn more gas.

Emissions by sector

There are eight main sectors of human activity responsible for greenhouse-gas emissions. Currently, the biggest is the generation of electricity by power plants that burn fossil fuels, but emissions from transportation are growing rapidly. The picture could change, especially if the destruction of tropical forests continues or the global use of fossil fuels is radically reduced.

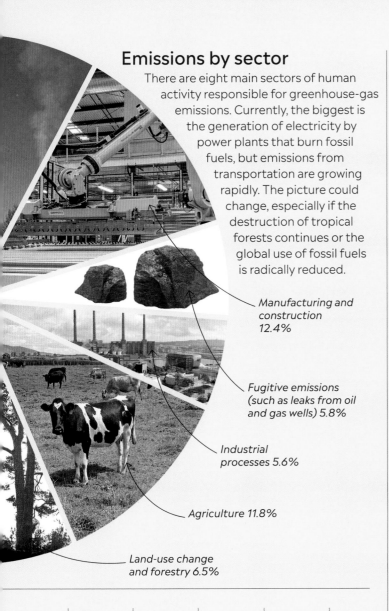

Manufacturing and construction 12.4%

Fugitive emissions (such as leaks from oil and gas wells) 5.8%

Industrial processes 5.6%

Agriculture 11.8%

Land-use change and forestry 6.5%

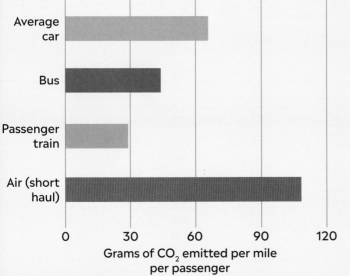

Grams of CO_2 emitted per mile per passenger

- Average car
- Bus
- Passenger train
- Air (short haul)

0 30 60 90 120

Transportation

Most forms of transportation rely on fossil fuels, but some use fuel more efficiently than others. Electric trains do not have to carry heavy fuel to power big engines. Air travel is the least fuel-efficient, especially over short distances, because of the power needed just to get airborne.

United States
19.8 tons p.a.
Population: 328 million

Canada
17.6 tons p.a.
Population: 38 million

Australia
16.5 tons p.a.
Population: 25 million

Japan
12.1 tons p.a.
Population: 127 million

Russia
10.4 tons p.a.
Population: 145 million

United Kingdom
9.1 tons p.a.
Population: 67 million

France
7.8 tons p.a.
Population: 67 million

China
6.6 tons p.a. Population: 1,393 billion

Brazil
2.8 tons p.a. Population: 210 million

India
1.9 tons p.a. Population: 1,353 billion

Carbon dioxide per person

The size of the flags above indicates the average amount of CO_2 released per annum (p.a.) by each citizen of a range of nations. They show that although China burns the most fossil fuel, its large population means that the average carbon footprint of each Chinese citizen is relatively small.

Timeline

Scientists study changes in Earth's climate by analyzing rock formations, ice cores, and plant growth over millions of years. The first weather records began in the 18th century, and methods of measuring atmospheric changes have only been developed in the last 150 years. This timeline tracks the events that have severely affected Earth's climate and the techniques used to study them.

Model of *Velociraptor*

250 million years ago (mya)
The biggest mass extinction in Earth's history destroys 96 percent of species, after massive volcanic eruptions releasing huge amounts of carbon dioxide (CO_2) increase the greenhouse effect, causing serious global warming and making life on Earth almost impossible.

250–65 mya
A warm, ice-free period leads to the age of the dinosaurs. This ends with another mass extinction, possibly caused by catastrophic volcanic activity coupled with the impact of a huge asteroid.

55 mya
A long period of global cooling begins, eventually leading to the ice ages that peak about 20,000 years ago. We are currently living in a warm phase compared to an ice age.

15,000 years ago
The last cold phase of the current ice age ends, and the vast ice sheets that cover much of North America, Europe, and northern Asia begin to melt.

13,000 years ago
Disruption of ocean currents caused by vast quantities of meltwater entering the north Atlantic causes a local temperature drop that lasts for 1,300 years. This is the period known as the "Younger Dryas."

8,000 years ago
CO_2 levels in the atmosphere rise by about 8 percent, while the first farmers are clearing and burning large areas of forest to create fields.

6,000 years ago
Drought brings an end to an 8,000-year monsoon climate in north Africa, turning tropical grasslands into vast desert—the Sahara.

1000 CE
Temperatures rise to the peak of the "Medieval Warm Period," whose climate is as warm as it is today. In Mexico, a prolonged drought causes the abandonment of many Mayan cities.

1430
Europe enters a "Little Ice Age" that lasts until the 19th century. The low temperatures cause widespread crop failures and famines and make rivers and canals freeze over each winter. This may be linked to increased volcanic activity producing ash clouds that partly reflected the sun's rays.

1607
At the first Frost Fair on the frozen Thames River in London, people flock to food stalls and sideshows on the thick ice. The last Frost Fair is in 1813, near the end of the Little Ice Age.

1703
Britain's most severe storm on record till then, known as the Great Storm, destroys many towns, killing 123 people on land, 8,000 at sea.

1709
British industrialist Abraham Darby invents a way of using coal to produce iron. This begins the intense use of fossil fuels as an industrial energy source. The resulting Industrial Revolution commences the large-scale increases in atmospheric CO_2.

1807
Coal gas provides the fuel for the first street-lighting system in London.

1815
The Indonesian volcano Tambora explodes in the largest volcanic eruption in recorded history. Airborne ash shading Earth causes the "year without a summer" of 1816.

1827
French mathematician Jean Baptiste Fourier discovers the greenhouse effect, by which gases in the atmosphere trap heat radiated from sun-warmed Earth.

1840
Swiss-born scientist Louis Agassiz proposes his theory of ice ages and realizes that northern Europe was once covered by an ice sheet.

Edison's light bulb, invented in 1879

1847
The world's first oil well is drilled at Baku, Azerbaijan.

1856
The first refinery for crude oil is at Ulaszowice, Poland.

1863
Irish scientist John Tyndall describes how water vapor can act as a greenhouse gas.

1882
American inventor Thomas Edison sets up the world's first commercial coal-fired electricity-generating station—the Pearl Street plant in New York City. It is used to supply power for the incandescent light bulbs invented by Edison in 1879.

1885
German engineer Karl Benz creates the first practical gas-engined car.

1895
Swedish physicist and chemist Svante Arrhenius suggests that adding CO_2 to Earth's atmosphere by burning coal might increase the greenhouse effect, causing global warming.

1908
In the United States, the Model T Ford goes into mass production, and car ownership starts to rise rapidly.

1920
Serbian scientist Milutin Milankovitch discovers how regular variations in Earth's orbit around the sun cause cycles of changing global temperature that are believed to be responsible for ice ages.

1931
After three years of drought, torrential rain falls for months in China. This causes the Yangtze River to flood catastrophically, rising up to 95 ft (29 m) above its usual level. As a result, 3.7 million people die through disease, starvation, or drowning. It is the most destructive climatic event in human history.

1932
Following years of drought, the desperately dry soil of the "Dust Bowl" in the American Midwest starts to blow away. The dust storms continue until 1939.

1939
British engineer Guy Stewart Callendar argues that observed global warming since the 19th century could be explained by a 10 percent rise in atmospheric CO_2. He suggests that a doubling of CO_2 in the atmosphere would bring about an average global temperature increase of 3.6°F (2°C).

1945
After rising steadily for about a century, global temperatures start to fall slowly because air pollution by soot and other particles partly obscures the sun.

1957
After discovering that the oceans cannot absorb all the extra CO_2 being created by the burning of fossil fuels, American oceanographer Roger Revelle warns that humanity is conducting a "large-scale geophysical experiment" by releasing greenhouse gases into the atmosphere.

1958
Charles Keeling starts recording atmospheric CO_2 concentrations, first in Antarctica and then in Hawaii. Over the following years, he records a steady long-term rise with annual fluctuations caused by Northern Hemisphere winters. The graph's line is described as the "sawtoothed curve."

1962
Russian climate expert Mikhail Budyko warns that the exponential growth of industrial civilization could cause drastic global warming within the next century.

1967
In the United States, geophysicists Syukuro Manabe and Richard Wetherald devise an early computer model of the global climate. This

A car crushed by a fallen tree, caused by the Great Storm of 1987 in the UK

agrees with Callendar's earlier suggestion that a doubling of atmospheric CO_2 could cause a global temperature rise of 3.6°F (2°C). Later computer models revise this figure to an even higher 5.4°F (3°C).

1968–1974
The Sahel region on the southern fringes of the Sahara in Africa suffers a seven-year drought. Millions die of starvation, and by the end of the drought, 50 million people are relying on food aid for survival.

1970
The worst tropical storm of the 20th century occurs in Bangladesh, where flooding caused by a 25-ft (7.5-m) storm surge in the Bay of Bengal kills up to 500,000 people.

1976–1977
Europe suffers a major drought, which in Britain is the worst for 250 years.

1977
Records show that global temperatures start to rise again after a reduction in soot emissions reduces the "global dimming" effect that air pollution is thought to have.

1982
Swiss physicist Hans Oeschger, working on atmospheric samples trapped in the ancient ice of the Greenland ice sheet, confirms the link between increasing atmospheric CO_2 and global warming.

1982–1983
Eastern Australia suffers its worst drought of the 20th century. It triggers the disastrous "Ash Wednesday" fires that kill more than 60 people around Victoria and South Australia.

1983–1985
Crop failures and famine brought about by civil war and a long drought in Ethiopia and Sudan kill 450,000 people, and millions more are made destitute.

1985
A drilling team at Vostok Station in central Antarctica produces an ice core that contains a 150,000-year record of temperature and atmospheric CO_2. This Vostok core shows that the levels of both have risen and fallen in remarkably close step and further proves the link between the two.

1987
The UK's most violent storm recorded since 1703 sweeps through southern England, uprooting more than 15 million trees.

1988
The UN asks for a high-level scientific assessment of climate change, which leads to the establishment of the Intergovernmental Panel on Climate Change (IPCC). Its role is to produce regular, detailed reports on the conclusions of climate scientists worldwide. The first report appears in 1990.

1990
A tropical cyclone (hurricane) in the Indian Ocean creates a storm surge 20 ft (6 m) high that sweeps up the Bay of Bengal and floods parts of the low-lying Bangladesh, causing around 148,000 deaths.

Ice cores at Vostok prove that atmospheric CO_2 levels affect global temperature

1990

In the United States, geophysicist Syukuro Manabe uses a computer model of world climate to show that global warming could weaken the Gulf Stream, possibly making northern Europe cooler rather than warmer.

1991

The eruption of Mount Pinatubo in the Philippines ejects a dust cloud into the atmosphere, making average global temperatures drop for two years.

1991–1992

Africa suffers its worst dry spell of the 20th century when 2.6 million sq miles (6.7 million sq km) are affected by drought.

1997

Wildfires in Indonesia destroy more than 1,160 sq miles (3,000 sq km) of forest, creating a vast cloud of pollution that adds as much CO_2 to the atmosphere as 30–40 percent of the world's fossil-fuel consumption.

1997

At a meeting in Kyoto, Japan, representatives of many countries agree to aim for a 5 percent cut in global greenhouse-gas emissions by 2012. The United States and Australia refuse to agree, but it becomes international law in 2005.

2000

Torrential rain and flooding hit the UK during the wettest autumn recorded in 300 years.

2001

The IPCC produces its third report, which shows that there is no longer any doubt among climate scientists that human activity is causing global climate change. The report includes the "hockey stick" graph showing temperatures over the past 1,000 years and the sharp upturn in the 20th century.

2002

The Larsen-B ice shelf near the tip of the Antarctic Peninsula disintegrates within 35 days, and 1,254 sq miles (3,250 sq km) of ice drift away to melt in the ocean.

Flooding after torrential rain due to Hurricane Katrina, 2005

2003

Europe experiences its most extreme heatwave for at least 500 years, with temperatures over 104°F (40°C); at least 30,000 people die as a result.

2004

A study published in the scientific journal *Nature* concludes that up to 52 percent of plant and animal species could face extinction because of climate change by the year 2050.

2004

Measurements of ocean currents associated with the Gulf Stream indicate that the flow has slowed since the 1960s. They suggest that the Gulf Stream might be under threat.

Forest in Australia burned down due to Australian bushfires in 2019–2020

2004–2005

A warm, snow-free winter forces most of the ski resorts in Washington and Oregon to shut down midway through the season.

2005

The British Antarctic Survey reveals that the massive West Antarctic ice sheet could be disintegrating—an event that could raise world sea levels by up to 16 ft (5 m).

2005

The Atlantic suffers the worst hurricane season on record, with 14 named storms. One of these, Hurricane Katrina, destroys much of New Orleans, Louisiana.

2006

Several of Greenland's glaciers are reported to be flowing much faster than in the past, indicating that the fringes of the Greenland ice sheet are reacting to global warming more quickly than had been predicted.

2007

China takes over from the United States as the world's biggest producer of greenhouse gases, even though China's emissions per person are only a quarter of those in the US. Much of the rise is caused by increased electricity generation by coal-fired power plants.

2007

Severe heatwaves hit southern Europe, with temperatures peaking at 114.8°F (46°C) in Greece, causing wildfires and deaths from heatstroke. Meanwhile, torrential rain strikes the UK, causing serious flooding. The intensity of the rainfall matches computer models of the changing climate.

2012

Arctic sea ice reaches the lowest extent since satellite records began in 1979.

2013

The IPCC's fifth report states that "Warming of the climate system is unequivocal."

2015

The Paris Agreement signed at the UN's climate change conference binds 195 nations to limiting climate change to below 3.6°F (2°C) warming.

2016

Global temperatures are the highest recorded, reaching 2°F (1.1°C) above pre-industrial times, due to further global warming and a large El Niño event in the Pacific.

2019–2020

Record-breaking heat and drought in Australia cause massive wildfires, causing the deaths of at least 34 people. Around 46 million acres (18.6 million ha) of forest are destroyed, and billions of animals die, driving some species to the brink of extinction.

Find out more

EVERY DAY THERE ARE ITEMS in the newspapers and other media about the latest scientific research into climate change. More detailed information about this work can be found on websites, in museums, and at institutions that specialize in this area. You can also find out more by doing some research of your own. Keep daily records of the weather or figure out how much energy you could save as a family by changing your way of life.

Museum trips

Many science museums and natural history museums have excellent exhibits covering topics raised in this book. They include London's Science Museum and Natural History Museum, Harvard University's Center for the Environment and Natural History Museum, and the Natural World Museum in San Francisco.

Visits and virtual visits

Your school may be able to arrange a visit to a wind farm (below), a hydroelectric station, a tidal barrage, a recycling plant, a zero-emissions housing development, an eco-city, or a local wildlife reserve. You can also go online for virtual tours and webcams that offer a fascinating glimpse of the latest research in action.

FIND OUT MORE

- This child-friendly site has fascinating facts about climate change: **https://kids.nationalgeographic.com/science/article/climate-change**
- The British Antarctic Survey shows life in the field: **https://www.bas.ac.uk**
- This guide contains articles, videos, and quizzes on climate change as part of the Geography course for kids: **https://www.bbc.co.uk/bitesize/guides/zx234j6/revision/1**
- NASA has a great collection of images (taken from space) on climate change: **https://earthobservatory.nasa.gov/**
- The magazine *New Scientist* has an extensive online report about climate change that is easy to read: **https://www.newscientist.com/article-topic/climate-change/**

WHAT'S YOUR EFFECT?

With online help, you can determine what kind of impact you are having on the climate and how you can minimize it. Calculate your carbon footprint with this website: **https://footprint.wwf.org.uk**. You'll also find great ideas on how to lessen your impact at these two sites: **www.energysavingtrust.org.uk/** and **https://www.energystar.gov/ia/products/globalwarming/downloads/.GoGreen_Activities%20508_compliant_small.pdf**

See Antarctica

The British Antarctic Survey currently has webcams at Halley and Rothera stations and on board RRS *James Clark Ross* and RRS *Ernest Shackleton*. There is also a webcam at King Edward Point, run by South Georgia's government. The US Antarctic Program also deploys people to Antarctica every year for research.

Glossary

Absorption
The process of intaking or absorbing something. Gases, such as CO_2, can be absorbed by liquids, such as water.

Albedo
Objects absorb some light and reflect the rest. The albedo of an object is the proportion of light that it reflects.

Alkaline
Describing a substance that contains particular minerals that make it opposite of acidic. Ocean water is naturally alkaline but absorbs so much CO_2 that it is becoming more acidic.

Anthracite
This is a very hard form of coal. It has the highest carbon count of all the different coal types and contains the fewest impurities.

Atmosphere
The layers of gases surrounding Earth or any other planet.

Bacteria
A large group of microscopic single-celled organisms, probably best known for causing disease, but also important for helping decomposition and recycling of substances.

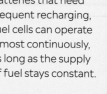

Bacteria

Biofuel
Fuel made from biomass, usually plants.

Biomass
Organic material from living organisms, such as plants and animals and their by-products, such as manure or garden waste.

Biosphere
The part of Earth's surface, ocean, and atmosphere that is inhabited by living things.

Carbohydrates
A large group of organic compounds, such as sugars and starches, that contain carbon, hydrogen, and oxygen. Carbohydrates are a key source of energy for animals and are found in many foods, such as potatoes and bread.

Carbon
A nonmetallic element that occurs in all organic compounds.

Carbonate
A salt made from carbonic acid.

Carbon dioxide (CO_2)
A colorless, odorless gas formed when carbon combines with oxygen. It is breathed out by animals and used by plants for photosynthesis. It is the main greenhouse gas responsible for global warming.

Carbon emissions
The CO_2 released, or emitted, into the atmosphere. Most of these emissions come from burning fossil fuels.

Carbon footprint
All of us emit CO_2 by burning fossil fuels, taking transportation that runs on fuel, or consuming goods that use these fuels in production and delivery. The amount of CO_2 a person's lifestyle emits is called the carbon footprint.

Data
A series of observations, measurements, or facts used to help draw conclusions or to back up research.

Drought
A long period of time with no rainfall.

Evaporate
To change from a liquid form to a gaseous form, such as water evaporating into water vapor.

Feedback
A reaction in response to a particular event.

Fertile
Describes land that has plenty of nutrients to enable plant growth.

Fluctuations
Irregular changes or variations of level or flow rate, as in temperatures or sea levels.

Fossil fuels
Carbon- or hydrocarbon-based fuels—such as coal, oil (derived products, such as gas and diesel), and natural gas—formed by the partial preservation of plant and animal remains. They release CO_2 when burned.

Fuel cell
An electrochemical energy converter. It produces electricity from outside supplies of fuel, such as hydrogen. Unlike batteries that need frequent recharging, fuel cells can operate almost continuously, as long as the supply of fuel stays constant.

Geology
The scientific study of the rocks and structure of Earth.

Gas pump

Glacier
A slowly moving mass of ice formed originally from compressed snow.

Hydrocarbon
An organic compound consisting entirely of hydrogen and carbon.

Ice sheet
Any large mass of glacial ice covering more than 19,000 sq miles (50,000 sq km). Greenland and Antarctica are ice sheets.

Ice shelf
A thick floating platform of ice that forms where an ice sheet or glacier flows down to a coastline and onto the ocean surface.

Parched land during a drought

Industrialization
The development of industry, such as manufacturing or construction, on a huge scale that relies on the creation of a huge amount of energy, usually by burning fossil fuels.

Infrared
A form of radiation detectable as heat, which has a wavelength longer than visible light but shorter than that of radio waves.

Insulation
Materials or techniques used to reduce the rate at which heat is conducted, such as through the walls of a building.

Interact
Two or more things acting in such a way that they influence one another.

Migration
Traveling from one area or country to another. Many animals, especially birds, migrate from one continent to another.

Molecule
Multiple atoms held together by chemical bonds. For example, a molecule of methane (natural gas) is made up of one carbon atom bonded to four hydrogen atoms.

Monsoon
A seasonal change of wind that affects the weather, especially in tropical regions where it causes wet and dry seasons.

Oxidize
To have a chemical reaction with the gas oxygen. For example, when carbon reacts with oxygen, it oxidizes and turns to CO_2.

Oxygen
A colorless, odorless gas, essential for the life of most organisms. Oxygen makes up about one-fifth of the air in Earth's atmosphere.

Ozone
A form of oxygen. The ozone layer helps block harmful radiation from the sun.

Particle
A minute bit of solid matter.

Permafrost
Ground that is permanently frozen.

Photosynthesis
The process by which plants and similar organisms use sunlight to make carbohydrate food from water and CO_2.

Plankton
Tiny living things that drift in the upper, sunlit layer of seas and lakes. They include plantlike organisms and animals.

Tropical rain forest

Pollution
Contamination with harmful substances.

Projection
A prediction based on known evidence and observations. Scientists gather data that allow them to make projections.

Radioactive
Describes an atomic nucleus that sends out waves of energy in the form of electromagnetic waves. The element uranium is radioactive.

Refrigerant
A fluid that is used to absorb heat and pump it out of refrigerators and freezers. In the past, refrigerants were often chlorofluorocarbons (CFCs)—powerful greenhouse gases that also destroy protective ozone in the atmosphere.

Renewable
Describes natural sources of energy that do not run out with use—such as wind, solar, or hydro-power—or any natural resource that can be sustained if carefully managed, such as forestry.

Sea level
The level of the sea surface in comparison to the land. All heights on land are measured in relation to average sea level.

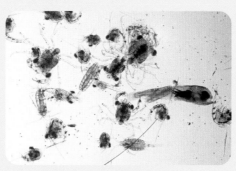
Plankton

Solar power
Energy produced from devices such as solar panels and solar collectors, which use sunlight to generate heat or electricity.

Solar radiation
The waves of light produced by the sun. Some of this energy is visible as sunlight.

Storm surge
A local rise in sea-level water caused by a low-pressure weather system, such as a hurricane or tropical cyclone.

Sustainable
Describes the management and use of natural resources at a steady level that is unlikely to damage the environment.

Temperate
A climate that is generally mild in temperature, with some rainfall.

Tropical
A climate that is very hot and often very wet or humid.

Tundra
Cold, treeless land fringing the polar regions, between the forests and the permanent ice.

Turbine
A machine that converts the movement of air or water into mechanical energy by using it to turn a rotor with blades.

Vegetation
Plant life, especially the plant life found in a particular region.

Water vapor
The invisible, gaseous form of water, which forms part of the atmosphere.

Index

Acknowledgments

The publisher would like to thank the following people with their help with making the book: Rebecca Painter and Kate Scarborough for pp.64–71; Ashwin Khurana for editorial assistance; Saloni Singh, Priyanka Sharma-Saddi, and Rakesh Kumar for the jacket; Kate Scarborough and Jim Green for the wallchart; and Joanna Penning for proofreading and indexing.

The publisher would like to thank the following for their kind permission to reproduce their photographs:
(Key: a-above; b-below/bottom; c-center; f-far; l-left; r-right; t-top)

2 Alamy Stock Photo: Adrian Muttitt (cr). Dreamstime.com: Stockphototrends (br). Getty Images: Corbis Documentary / Steve Austin (r); Stone / Peter Cade (bl). NASA: (tl). 3 NASA: JPL-Caltech AIRS Project (c). 4 Dreamstime.com: Markus Gann (tl). Science Photo Library: Institute Of Oceanographic Sciences / NERC (r). 5 Getty Images: DigitalVision / Jose Luis Pelaez Inc (r). 6 Dorling Kindersley: NASA (tr). 7 Getty Images: UniversalImagesGroup / Universal History Archive (br). BAS: Karl Tuplin (tl). 9 Dorling Kindersley: NASA (cb). Getty Images: The Image Bank Unreleased / Jim Sugar (tl). Science Photo Library: Brian Gadsby (tr). 10 Alamy Stock Photo: Giedrius Stakauskas (bl). 10-11 Dreamstime.com: Orlando Florin Rosu / Orla (c) Boonchuay Iamsumang (tl). 11 Dreamstime.com: Saskia Massink / Saspartout (clb); Piboon Srimak / Piboon (br). Science Photo Library: Bernhard Edmaier (r). 12 Science Photo Library: David Hay Jones (tr). 13 Alamy Stock Photo: Globe Stock (tr). Environmentalism for Nuclear Energy: (br). Getty Images: De Agostini Editorial / DEA / Albert Ceolan (tl). 14 Dreamstime.com: Lucy Brown (bl); Markus Gann (tr). 14-15 Getty Images: AFP / Arlan Naeg (c). 15 © 2008 by The Trustees of Columbia University in the City of New York, Lamont-Doherty Earth Observatory: (r). 16-17 Science Photo Library: British Antarctic Survey (c). 17 Getty Images: Corbis Documentary / Steve Austin (r). Science Photo Library: British Antarctic Survey (cl); Mauro Fermariello (tr). 18 Dreamstime.com: SimonDannhauer (tl). 18-19 Getty Images: Corbis News / Orjan F. Ellingvag (c). 19 Getty Images: Universal Images Group / Avalon (tc, b). NASA: NASA Worldview, Earth Observing System Data and Information System (EOSDIS) (bl). 20 Alamy Stock Photo: Jim West (cr). Dorling Kindersley: Oxford University Museum of Natural History / Neil Fletcher / The Oxford University Museum of Natural History (cra). Getty Images: Bettmann (br). 21 Alamy Stock Photo: Imaginechina Limited (crb). Getty Images: Bloomberg / Carina Johansen (l); Westend61 (cla). Science Photo Library: John Clegg (cr). 22-23 Shutterstock.com: Mislik (cl). 22 Alamy Stock Photo: Philip Duff (crb). Dreamstime.com: Photomall (clb).

Shutterstock.com: Pavel L Photo and Video (cb). 23 Shutterstock.com: OlegDoroshin (bl); Bell Ka Pang (cb). 24 Dreamstime.com: Sergeychernov (cla). FLPA: Nigel Cattlin (clb). Science Photo Library: Tony Hertz / Agstockusa (bl). 25 Alamy Stock Photo: TTstudio (cla). Getty Images: Alex Livesey (clb). Science Photo Library: Simon Fraser / Northumbrian Environmental Management Ltd (r). 26 Getty Images: AFP / Joel Robine (cl). Reuters: Mario Anzuoni (cla). 26-27 Getty Images: AFP / Bertrand Guay (c). 27 Alamy Stock Photo: Cavan Images / Aurora Photos / Ted Wood (tc). Getty Images: Gamma-Rapho / Greenpeace / Daniel Beltra (tl). NASA: NOAA (cr). NASA's Earth Observatory: (cr). Shutterstock.com: EPA / Maxim Shipenkov (br). 28 Alamy Stock Photo: Padi Prints / Troy TV Stock (bl). Dreamstime.com: Tony Skerl (clb). Shutterstock.com: MCL Yingling (cla). 28-29 Alamy Stock Photo: Robertharding / Tony Waltham (c). Dreamstime.com: Nataliya Nazarova (bc). 29 Alamy Stock Photo: Science History Images / Jessica Wilson (br). Bridgeman Images: © Wolfgang Neeb (crb). 31 Alamy Stock Photo: Agencia Fotograficzna Caro / Robert Seeberg (tr). Dreamstime.com: Philip Dickson / Psdphotography (cra). Getty Images: AFP / Adrien Barbier (cla); Handout / Dan International Australia (tr). Reuters: Volvo Ocean Race / ABN AMRO ONE / Handout (crb). 32-33 Alamy Stock Photo: IAN Fairbrother (c). 32 Alamy Stock Photo: BIOSPHOTO / Christoph Gerigk (br); dpa picture alliance / National Oceanography Centre (clb). 33 Ecoscene: Stuart Donachie (cr). Science Photo Library: European Space Agency (tc); Dr Ken Macdonald (clb); Institute Of Oceanographic Sciences / NERC (bc). 34 Alamy Stock Photo: Ernie Janes (tr). SuperStock: Minden Pictures / Michael & Patricia Fogden (cl). 35 Getty Images: Alexis Rosenfeld. 36 Alamy Stock Photo: Design Pics Inc / Alaska Stock Images (bl). Dreamstime.com: Vlada Koliada (c). 36-37 Alamy Stock Photo: Kevin Schafer (c). 37 Alamy Stock Photo: NatPar Collection (br). Dreamstime.com: Ondřej Prosický (cra). Shutterstock.com: Splashdown / Michael Nolan (cr). 38 Science Photo Library: Patrick Dumas / Look At Sciences (cl). 38-39 NASA. 39 Getty Images: The Image Bank Unreleased / Jim Sugar (cra). 40 Alamy Stock Photo: Gary Cook (cla). Science Photo Library: Ian Hooton (cr). 40-41 Dreamstime.com: Chuyu (b). 41 Alamy Stock Photo: AB Forces News Collection / Staff Sgt. Daniel J. Martinez (cra). Getty Images / iStock: ZayacSK (cr). 42 Getty Images: Logan Mock-Bunting (bl). Getty Images / iStock: Toa 5 (cl). 42-43 Alamy Stock Photo: Zakir Hossain Chowdhury (c). 43 Alamy Stock Photo: Design Pics Inc / Alaska Stock LLC (cr); Hemis.fr / Philippe Bourseiller (clb); Pavel Filatov (tr). Dreamstime.com: Tony Craddock (tr). 44-45 Getty Images: Barcroft Media / Anuwar Ali Hazarika (c). 45 Alamy Stock Photo: EFE News Agency / Esteban Biba (tr); FEMA (cr). Dreamstime.com: Manop Lohkaew (cra). 46-47 Alamy Stock

Photo: Nathaniel Noir (c). 46 Getty Images: AFP / Rodrigo Arangua (crb); Corbis Documentary / Douglas Peebles (cr). 47 Alamy Stock Photo: Joerg Boethling (br); Andy Sutton (clb). Getty Images: Corbis Historical / Gideon Mendel (tr). 48 Alamy Stock Photo: dpa picture alliance / Daniel Reinhardt (bc). Getty Images: Anadolu Agency / Arnaud Bouissou / COP21 (cl); The Image Bank Unreleased / Howard Davies (clb). 48-49 Alamy Stock Photo: ZUMA Press, Inc. / Andre Malerba (c). 49 Alamy Stock Photo: Rob Arnold (c); Edward Parker (ca). Shutterstock.com: AP / Michael Sohn (br). 50 Getty Images / iStock: sarkophoto (bl). 50-51 Getty Images: Chien-min Chung (c). 51 Getty Images: AFP / TT News Agency / Erik Simander (cla); DigitalVision / Jose Luis Pelaez Inc (br). 52-53 Dreamstime.com: Salih Arikan (soil); Milllda (pavement). 53 Alamy Stock Photo: Rob Crandall (tr); UPI / Keizo Mori (cr). Dreamstime.com: Johncarnemolla (cr). Science Photo Library: (tr); TRL Ltd. (cra); Steve Allen (cr). 54-55 Shutterstock.com: craig coker (b). 54 Getty Images / iStock: Tim Graham (ca). Shutterstock.com: Gary Saxe (cla). 55 Dreamstime.com: Anny Ben (c). Marine Current Turbines TM Ltd: (tr). Science Photo Library: Bjorn Svensson (ca). 56 Alamy Stock Photo: Mark Boulton (cla). Dreamstime.com: Xxlphoto (bl). 56-57 Getty Images: The Image Bank Unreleased / Alison Wright (bc). 57 Alamy Stock Photo: Ashley Cooper (cla). Dreamstime.com: Marco De Heus (cra). PunchStock: Purestock (b). 58-59 Alamy Stock Photo: Westend61 GmbH / Werner Dieterich (c). 58 Alamy Stock Photo: Mark Boulton (clb); Bruno Rodrigues Baptista da Silva (bc). Getty Images: Ted Kinsman (c). 59 Alamy Stock Photo: Hans Blossey (cb). Getty Images: Universal Images Group / View Pictures (cra). Shutterstock.com: Rawpixel.com (tr). 60-61 Getty Images: Archive Photos / Smith Collection / Gado (b). 60 Alamy Stock Photo: Dennis Cox (ca). Dreamstime.com: Sorin Colac (cra). Getty Images / iStock: E+ / georgeclerk (cla). 61 Getty Images / iStock: Imagebroker / Arco Images / Scholz, T (cla); Justin Kase zsixz (tl); Adrian Muttitt (cl). 62 Dreamstime.com: Sjors737 (bl). Getty Images: (bc). Shutterstock.com: Iakov Filimonov (cl). 62-63 Getty Images: Stone / Peter Cade (c). 63 Getty Images: Tetra Images, LLC / JGI / Tom Grill (cra). Shutterstock.com: Stockphototrends (crb); Chun Ju Wu (cra). Shutterstock.com: Sterling Images (tr). 64 Dreamstime.com: Luke Wendling (cla). 66 Dorling Kindersley: Science Museum, London (cr). 67 Getty Images: Hulton Archive / Georges De Keerle (cra). Science Photo Library: Munoz-Yague / Eurelios (br). 68 Alamy Stock Photo: Janine Powell Photography (cra). Getty Images: AFP / Pool (bl). 69 Alamy Stock Photo: GM Photo Images (br); David Kilpatrick (tr). 70 Alamy Stock Photo: Science History Images / Photo Researchers (cl). Dreamstime.com: Ahmad Marzuky (cr). 71 Dreamstime.com: Chan Yee Kee (c).

All other images © Dorling Kindersley
For further information see: www.dkimages.com